THE BALANCED VIOLINIST

TECHNIQUE COMPANION TO KALEIDOSCOPES BOOK 1

by Elise Winters

ISBN 978-1-959675-06-8

About the Author

Elise Winters began her violin studies at the age of four in the cradle of the Suzuki community in Frederick, Maryland. She continued with internationally renowned Suzuki teacher Ronda Cole and with Elisabeth Adkins, associate concertmaster of the National Symphony Orchestra. A graduate *summa cum laude* of Rice University in English and Music and a University of Texas Presidential Scholar with a Master of Social Work, she has performed with the Austin Symphony Orchestra for more than two decades and is a widely admired chamber musician and soloist.

Elise has extensive training in both Suzuki and Kodály methodologies. Her interests extend to developmental psychology, linguistics, cognition, communication, biomechanics, and ecstatic dance. Her diverse background has placed her in a unique position to write an inter-disciplinary, child-focused violin method.

Elise resides in Austin, Texas. Whenever she is not teaching or performing, she can be found enjoying Indian curry, sipping a latte at Monkey Nest Coffee, or dancing.

Acknowledgments

It is a pleasure to express my sincere gratitude to the many people who have contributed to Kaleidoscopes.

To my students, who have been my greatest teachers. Your earnest efforts provided unerring guidance for the sequence of technique and the final selection of songs. In particular I want to recognize William, Emily, Gloria, Elana, Sophia, Darwin, Delphine, Anayi, and Meilan. Your joyful hearts have left an indelible imprint on my own and helped to infuse these materials with creativity and love.

A special appreciation to the beloved students who lent their talents to the photography in the book: Eva, Nisha, Anushka, Katie, Weiran, Grace, Roger, Jia-Ray, and Sophia.

Numerous kindred spirits enriched the development of this approach. I am grateful to Robin Johnson, Kay Mueller, Nicole Ballinger, Lindsay Szczesny, Ruth Roland, Emily Rolka, and Erika Walczak. Your encouragement and shared passion have been a constant source of strength.

I owe a great debt of gratitude to Shinichi Suzuki, who forever changed what is possible for children and families. To Ronda Cole, without whom I would not be who I am. And to Klondike Steadman, without whom this book would not exist.

To the many additional teachers who have embraced this path with open arms and a willingness to explore, I honor your courage and commitment to nurturing young hearts and minds.

Last, my heartfelt thanks to my partner Chris, for always providing a safe harbor for my spirit. Your caring and constant support have given me the strength to go beyond my own limitations. Thank you for believing in me.

Table of Contents

Note to the Reader

This book provides the essential tools to establish posture and fluency for a young violinist. It is designed as the companion book to Kaleidoscopes Book 1, but may also be used independently.

The Kaleidoscopes Book 1 repertoire recordings are available to stream on all major platforms.

Please visit YouTube.com/discoverviolin for many of the exercises within this book. The Kaleidoscopes website, discoverviolin.org, also includes articles, videos, and other resources.

Please convey your appreciation for the research reflected in these pages by refraining from photo-copying, scanning, or otherwise reproducing the book, in whole or in part, without prior permission. Contact the publisher at business@discoverviolin.org.

CHAPTER 1

BEFORE THE
FIRST LESSON

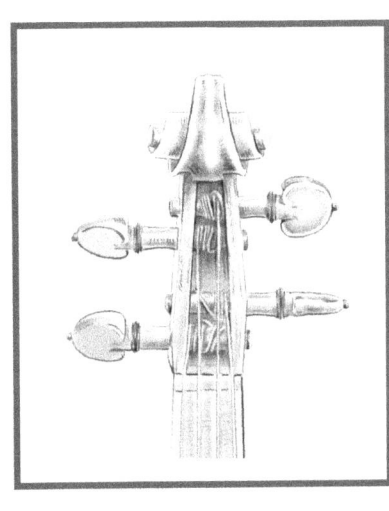

IN THIS SECTION:

Being an Excellent Practice Parent

If you are reading this book because you have just enrolled your child in violin lessons, congratulations on this big step! And if you are a friend or family member who will be serving as a trusted practice helper, this book is for you, as well!

If your child is 8 years old or younger, your first 5–6 lessons will be just you and the teacher. You will learn to play a few songs on the violin. This will help you to understand the skills involved and give you empathy for any challenges that may arise with posture, fatigue, and making a beautiful sound.

As the child watches you practice at home, it will increase their motivation to play. Once they begin, it will give you authority in their eyes: they see that you have done it already, so they will have more respect for your corrections.

You will eventually need to know almost everything about beginning violin technique. Since you will be your child's at-home violin coach, the quality of your child's progress will correlate directly to the quality of the corrections you are making with them!

No pressure, right?

It's okay. You can do this. You don't have to teach new material — you just need to assist your child in mastering each lesson's activities. Your teacher will work with you during lessons to help you 1) understand what has been covered, and 2) be able to work confidently with your child.

Setting Up Your Practice Space

The ideal practice space is a dedicated place in your home which is a bit separated from the daily commotion.

Many of the skills your child is working on will require intent listening, which is harder to do when there are external noises present. A set-aside area will also help you to separate mentally from your own work and household activities.

Your practice area really only needs a few items — the essentials are a piano and bench, violin materials, a chair for you, and a small table or desk. Dedicate some open floor space for active movement breaks, and avoid couches and cozy chairs that may be a little too inviting.

> Avoid couches and cozy chairs that may be a little too inviting.

While occasional interruptions from other family members are normal, do your best to handle such needs in advance so that you are free to focus your full attention on your child. Leave your phone outside of the room if possible, so it is not pulling on your attention.

Take time to plan your mindset as well as the practice activities so that this time is consistently positive. Treat your practice time as a special time for you to share with your child, and bring creativity and joy to each practice.

Take Notes at Lessons

As the practice parent, one of your roles will be to take notes during the lesson. These notes will be essential as you practice at home with your child. Even if you do not consider yourself musical, there are many reasons that you are the perfect person to fulfill this role!

- The process of organizing your thoughts on paper will enhance your own understanding. You can discover any areas you need to clarify while the teacher is still available to answer questions.

- Since the teacher's hands are often quite busy during the lesson, you'll be able to capture much more detail than they can.

- You can capture information in whatever way is clearest to you.

- The teacher is free to use the full lesson for teaching, rather than taking valuable time to stop and write things down.

Create a violin notebook to bring to each lesson. If someone else brings your child to the lesson, make sure this person has the notebook and knows how to take good notes for you.

When you take notes, include:

1. *How* the activity was presented
2. *Exact details* of position and execution
3. *Exact language* that the teacher used. The exact words are important.
4. How to *guide and correct* the new skill

You will want to video record new skills (mark a $\boxed{V}$ in your notebook beside these).

Please keep your phone away at all other times, though; it's easy to get distracted and miss key points of the lesson. Your whole-hearted attention in the lesson honors the space of the lesson and supports your child's learning.

Build Your Child's Musical Experiences

A child's early years are the most receptive time for developing both spoken language and music. This is the best time for your child to become a "native speaker" in a variety of musical styles.

Classical music has a wider musical vocabulary and more complex structure than many other types of music. Be sure to include this genre in your family's regular daily listening, along with other musical styles that you enjoy.

Your child will need enough repetition of various pieces to get to know them deeply, like a good friend. This means listening to the same pieces frequently ... ideally within a week or two, while the memory is still fresh. Over time your child will begin to discern the musical "storyline," harmonies, and other details.

The musical landscapes you share with your child will become a part of who they are.

Listen Daily to the Kaleidoscopes Recording

Children learn the language of music the same way they learn their native language. To create an immersive environment for early violin study, your child needs to hear their repertoire music *daily*.

Two kinds of listening are valuable: 1) Playing the music softly in the background; and 2) Actively listening to (and sometimes singing along with) the songs.

Parents are often surprised to learn that listening is twice as important as practicing. Music teachers can readily observe this. The more you listen, the faster your child will progress.

Purchase a good-quality speaker for several areas of your home, and try to play the recording twice daily. Always play the entire album; this will give your child the necessary preparation for the harder songs at the end of the book.

Make sure to listen as a family, rather than simply having your child listen on their own. The experience of singing together as a family will help connect your child more deeply to the music.

As an adult, you will quickly become familiar with these simple songs, since you are already "fluent" in the language of Western music. However, do keep playing the recording, because it will take your child *much* longer! Trying to learn a song before it is imprinted in their mind is like trying to put together a puzzle of an object they've never seen before.

As they continue listening, your child is internalizing not just "how the song goes," but also the piano score, musical details, and tone. As with learning a language, they need to learn not just the words, but also the subtleties of expression.

Daily Repertoire Listening Plan

	Kaleidoscopes Repertoire	Classical & Other Music
Getting ready in the morning	❑	❑
Quiet playtime (morning)	❑	❑
Driving to and from school	❑	❑
Free play at school (*many preschool teachers will gladly do this*)	❑	❑
Quiet playtime (afternoon)	❑	❑
Dinnertime (violin portion)	❑	❑
Bathtime	❑	❑
Getting ready for bed	❑	❑
Errands in the car	❑	❑
Other: _____	❑	❑

CLASSICAL MUSIC PLAYLIST

- *Use this list as a starting point in developing a library of classical music that your child will get to know well.*
- *Listen to several selections each week (make a playlist), and listen to this at least four times during the week.*
- *Return to earlier selections after a few months so the child can continue absorbing them.*

	Baroque & Ancient		Classical		Romantic and Beyond		
✓	Antonio Vivaldi The Four Seasons		Ludwig van Beethoven Für Elise		Peter Tchaikovsky Serenade for Strings		Gustave Holst The Planets
	J.S. Bach Brandenburg Concertos		Franz Joseph Haydn String Quartet Op.76 no.3, "Emperor"		Aaron Copland Hoedown from "Rodeo"		Felix Mendelssohn Overture to "A Midsummer Night's Dream"
	J.S. Bach First Cello Suite		Ludwig van Beethoven Pastoral Symphony		Henri Wieniawski Scherzo Tarantelle		Claude Debussy Clair de la Lune
	J.S. Bach Concerto for Two Violins in D Minor		G. Rossini Overture to "William Tell"		C. Saint-Saëns Carnival of the Animals		Aram Khachaturian Sabre Dance
	J.S. Bach Toccata and Fugue		Ludwig van Beethoven Moonlight Sonata		Edvard Grieg Piano Concerto in A Minor		Antonio Bazzini Ronde des Lutins
	Arcangelo Corelli 12 Concerto Grossi, op.6		Wolfgang Amadeus Mozart String Quartet "The Hunt"		George Gershwin Rhapsody in Blue		Johann Strauss Overture to "Die Fledermaus"
	Antonio Vivaldi Guitar Concerto in D		Gioacchino Rossini Overture to "La Gazza Ladra"		Pablo de Sarasate Carmen Fantasy		Edvard Grieg Peer Gynt Suite
	Giovanni da Palestrina Missa Pape Marcelli		Wolfgang Amadeus Mozart Overture to "The Marriage of Figaro"		Fritz Kreisler Tambourin Chinois		Alexander Borodin String Quartet no.2
	Remo Giazotto Adagio in G Minor for Strings and Organ		Wolfgang Amadeus Mozart Violin Concerto No.3 in G Major		Modest Mussorgsky Pictures at an Exhibition (orchestra version)		Claude Debussy La Mer

Talk with your child each week about one of the pieces they are hearing. Help them learn the name, the composer's name (first and last), and an interesting fact. Share these with your teacher at each violin lesson.

Why Daily Practice?

Practice every day for 15–30 minutes. For young children, do 2–3 sessions of 5–10 minutes.

Daily practice gives the following benefits:

1. It tells the child that violin study is important – both in general, and to you.

2. Your child will make good progress and see the results of their hard work. This will give them a positive feeling about practicing.

3. Daily practice will become a routine for them. Their mind and body will adjust to this rhythm. This builds the foundation of mental and emotional discipline.

4. You will adjust to this routine as well, so you both reinforce each other.

However, when you skip practice:

1. It tells the child that practice is optional. As a result, they will want to practice when *they* want to practice.

2. It tells the child that studying violin is nice but not very important. They won't be willing to work as hard and will progress more slowly. They will become an average player, but will not connect their average results to inconsistent practicing. When they hear another player their age who is much better than them, they will think that child simply "is" better.

3. Whatever was learned during the previous practice will erode during the day off. After another missed day it will be nearly gone. The child will conclude that practicing does not yield results. When they do practice from time to time, their heart will not be in it, because it seems pointless.

4. You yourself will get out of the routine! Other things will begin to take the place of practice.

5. Your child will not reap the full developmental benefits of playing violin. These benefits include greater mental acuity, language and math aptitude, physical coordination, and spatial awareness ... as well as discipline and perseverance, to name just a few.

6. Your money on lessons will not be well spent. Violin lessons are an excellent investment, but only if you practice and achieve results.

Paradoxically, practice — like physical exercise — gets easier to do when it is an everyday routine. It will simply become part of your daily rhythm.

As Suzuki said, "You only have to practice on the days you eat."

Is My Child Old Enough to Practice Independently?

Violin is complex both physically and cognitively. There is a high level of detail and precision in multiple dimensions; integrating the many skills requires planning and psychological insight ... as well as a second set of eyes.

Your child will need your full, undivided attention as they practice. Be creative, have fun, and make violin practice a delightful and rewarding time you and your child share together!

If your child is age 8–11, they may already be quite responsible and independent in many ways, but they will still need you during the first two years. Imagine how difficult it would be for them to design a lesson plan for a younger sibling! This is the kind of challenge they will face when they practice violin independently.

A very mature child may begin gradually transitioning to independent practicing between ages 10–12, after completing Book 2. A good-quality transition takes approximately two years.

Essential Violin Materials

Violin

A good violin shop will fit your child for the correct size violin. Ask them to err on the smaller side. This will provide greater comfort and promote better posture.

Purchase your violin *only* from a specialized music shop. Most low-priced violins sold online are made of inferior materials which no amount of repair can remedy.

Bow

The bow should be stored with the hairs quite loose, so they do not cause the stick to warp (lose its shape). The hair should be tightened only *slightly* before playing — it should still feel quite pliable, and the bow should retain its arc shape.

Rosin

You will find this in the pocket of your violin case. Made from pine sap, rosin allows the bow to grip the violin strings.

Sponge (or Shoulder Rest)

A PolyPad™ sponge is ideal for most young students. A Kun-style shoulder rest may also be a good option if your child has a longer neck.

Nail Clippers

Keep an extra pair in the violin case, in order to trim the fingernails before each practice.

Chinrest

If the violin does not feel comfortable even after a few weeks, or if the head angle looks awkward to you, ask your teacher about trying a Wittner chinrest.

Carpet

Practicing on carpet protects the violin & bow in case of slips, and will help your child to refrain from gripping tightly.

Electronic Metronome - Tuner

Ask your violin shop to suggest a metronome-tuner that has a loud wood-block sound rather than a beep. You will want a dedicated device rather than a phone app, so that it will available to your child when you are out of the room.

Music Stand

You and your child will both appreciate having a solid-desk, Manhasset-style stand rather than a more flimsy "wire" one. The solid desk holds more music, is easier to write on, and can be used for other purposes, such as a podium or laptop stand.

Caring for the Violin & Bow

Violin Care

The *bridge* of the violin is not attached to the top of the violin; it is held there only by the strings' tension and can move easily if bumped. When you tune the violin, check that the bridge is perfectly upright. *If you discover it leaning, immediately request help from your teacher or the violin shop, to avoid warping the bridge.* If on occasion you discover the violin more out of tune than usual, it is often because the bridge was bumped.

Keep the violin at a consistent temperature and avoid extremes of heat and humidity. Never leave the violin in the car, and do not place it near a heating duct. Dry air will cause the wood to shrink, and the pegs may become loose in the pegbox.

Protect the violin from bumps, and practice on carpet in case of unexpected falls. Teach your child to always walk with the violin in rest position and how to move slowly and carefully when holding it.

Before putting away the violin, remove the shoulder rest and use a soft cotton cloth to clean off the rosin dust. When closing the case, be sure that the top of the case does not press down on the bridge of the violin.

Bow Care

Before playing, tighten the bow hair using the screw, *only until the hair is about a pencil's width from the stick.* The stick should retain its "smile" shape.

Sometimes a few hairs are looser than the rest. Tighten the bow only until the *ribbon* of hair (not including flyaways) are a pencil-width from the stick. Allow the loose strands to remain, or your teacher can use scissors to remove them.

If your child tightens their own bow, check their work; a child who is distracted may turn the screw as far as possible without realizing it.

After practicing, loosen the screw until there is no pressure on the hair. Forgetting to do this may permanently damage the bow.

Vigorously rub rosin onto the bow hairs once a week. Clean the rosin from the violin strings before putting it away so the rosin does not become caked onto the varnish.

Avoid touching the bow hair with your skin, since the natural oils will create a slick spot on the hair. The bowhold thumb may touch the edge of the hair during normal playing (and when practicing bowholds); this is fine.

How Do You Tune It?

Tuning your child's violin will require a little knowledge of music theory. If you don't have a musical background, don't worry — just do your best to understand this article, and ask your teacher to explain whatever doesn't quite make sense.

Naming the notes

The notes of the scale ascend the alphabet from A to G. Each successive A is higher than the previous one (see the piano illustration below). This repeating eight-note span is called an *octave*.

To help musicians refer to individual notes, each octave is labeled numerically from 1 (the lowest) to 7 (the highest). While the piano has all seven octaves, the violin has a four-octave range.

The strings of the violin are G3, D4, A4 and E5. The G string of the violin is a little left of center on the piano, and each successive string is five notes higher.

Half steps and whole steps

On the piano, each key is *one half-step* from the note directly above or below, whether that key is black or white. Sometimes there are two white keys in a row; these are similarly a half-step apart. White keys that are separated by one black key are *one whole step* apart.

The white keys have *natural* note names — e.g. A♮ ("A natural") or "A" for short. By contrast, black keys have *flat* (♭) or *sharp* (♯) names. For example, the black key between A and B can be called either A♯ or B♭.

The strings of the violin are all natural notes. So if you're tuning A string and your electronic tuner shows G♯ or A♭, this means you're one half step too low.

Similarly, if the tuner shows A♯ or B♭ then you are one half-step too high.

Just because the tuner is showing you a green light doesn't mean you're in tune. You also need to check the *exact* note name. If the tuner says A♯ and you're tuning A string, you've got some work to do.

First steps to tuning the violin

To tune the violin, place the tuner next to you and pluck any string. To get a more stable reading on the tuner, use the bow rather than plucking. Don't worry about using correct technique; just draw the bow in a comfortable way. You can place the violin on your lap or on a flat surface in front of you.

Centering the needle

If you are tuning the A string and the display reads "A4," you are on the right track! The next step is to get the string *exactly* in tune.

Your display may have a needle which moves left or right, depending on whether the note is too low or too high. It may alternately use red or green lights for the same purpose.

Use the *fine tuners* (on the violin tailpiece) to make small adjustments to the pitch. Tightening the tuners will raise the pitch; loosening lowers the pitch. Adjust each screw until the tuner indicates that the note is in tune.

Using the pegs

The *pegs* are used for larger adjustments to the pitch (more than one whole step), while the fine tuners make smaller adjustments (less than a whole step). If you must use the pegs, only a tiny turn is usually needed. On a full-size violin, even just a quarter-turn is *four* whole-steps!

To raise the pitch using the pegs, turn the peg toward the pegbox. This will wind more of the string onto the peg, which stretches the string more tightly. To lower the pitch, turn the peg away from the scroll, reducing the tension.

The pegs may sometimes be difficult to turn; don't be afraid to use a strong force. However, be ready for

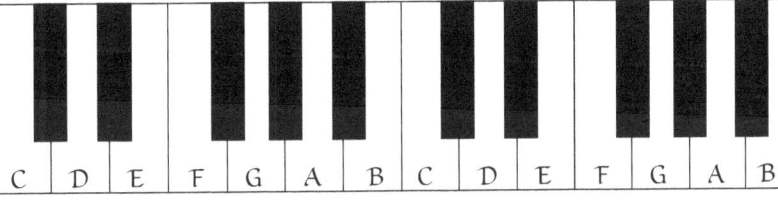

REMINDER: Before playing, tighten the bow hair using the screw, *only until the hair is about a pencil's width from the stick*. The stick should retain its "smile" shape.

Sometimes a few hairs are looser than the rest. Tighten the bow only until the *ribbon* of hair (not including flyaways) are a pencil-width from the stick.

After practicing, loosen the screw until there is no pressure on the hair.

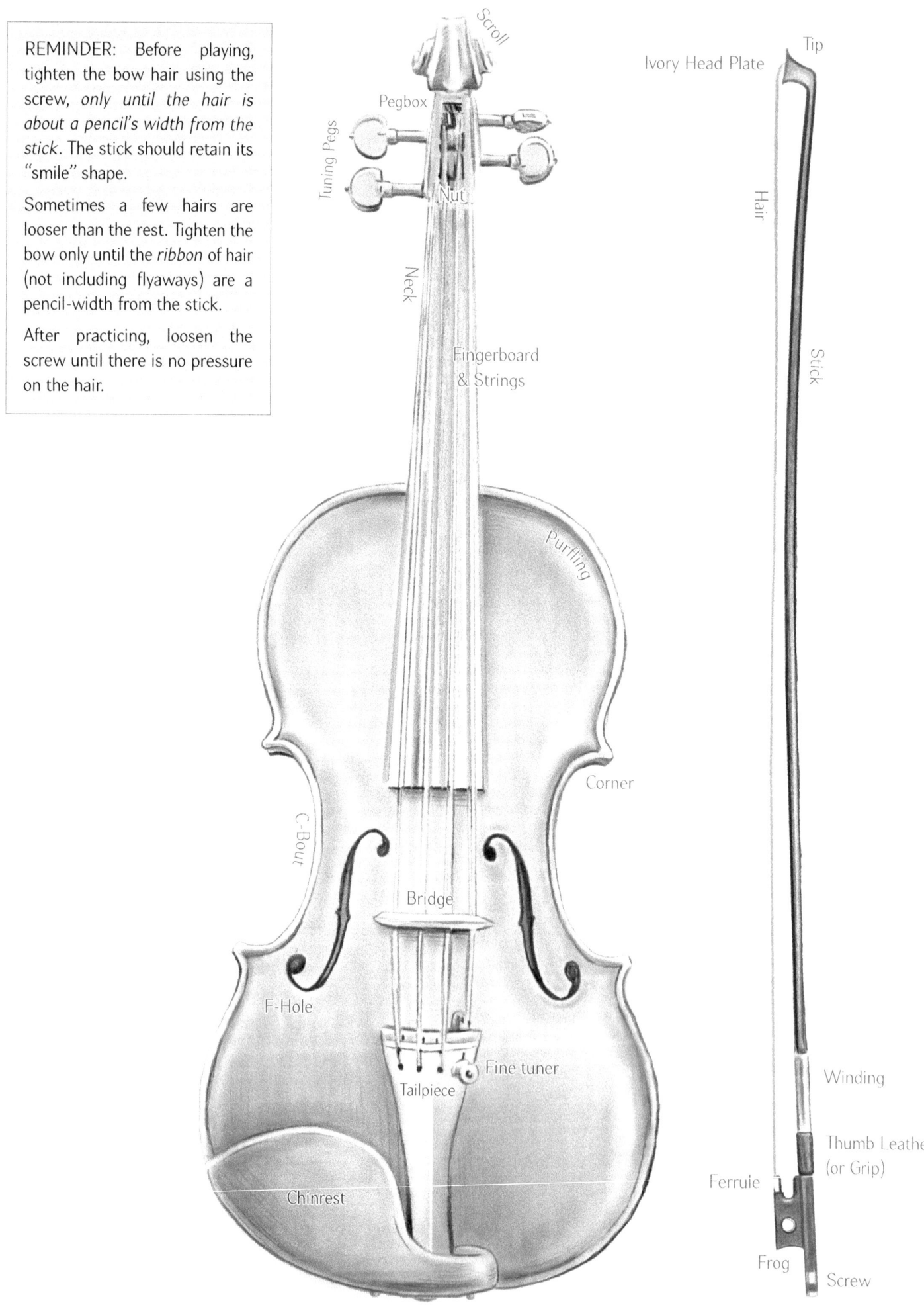

Scroll

Ivory Head Plate

Tip

Pegbox

Tuning Pegs

Nut

Hair

Neck

Stick

Fingerboard & Strings

Purfling

Corner

C-Bout

Bridge

F-Hole

Fine tuner

Winding

Tailpiece

Thumb Leather (or Grip)

Ferrule

Chinrest

Frog

Screw

End Button

when the peg begins to move, because you should immediately stop turning it. You don't want to do more than ¼ turn at a time.

The pegs have a tendency to wiggle themselves loose while you're tuning. For this reason, you should exert a little *inward* force as you turn, as though you are screwing the pegs into the holes.

What if I break something?

Tuning a violin is low-risk. Even if a string snaps, they are inexpensive ... although it is a bit startling. Give yourself room to make mistakes; you don't have to be a rocket scientist to decently tune a violin.

The most important thing is to avoid tightening the string too rapidly. If you overshoot the correct note and the string reaches its maximum stress point, it will break. This is more likely to happen on the E string than the others, since the E is already a high-tension string.

Again, it is okay if this happens – it's just inconvenient and you may lose a day of practicing until you get to the shop.

Tune the violin daily

Tune the violin before every practice, even if you don't think it needs it. It will probably take some time to hold its tuning, especially if the strings are new or if it hasn't been played regularly for awhile.

Begin to have your child participate in tuning the violin once they are old enough. They can use the tuners, but don't allow them to use the pegs until they are more advanced.

How (Not) to Use the Printed Music

Your child should learn the Kaleidoscopes songs by ear from the recording. This is accomplished by listening daily to the recording and singing along as often as possible.

Following Along in the Music

The pictorial notation in the book is intended as a visualization tool only. Singing the song while pointing to the pictorial notation is an good tool for kinesthetic learning, especially for very young children. Following the notes in tempo will be harder for them than you might expect! Seeing the rising and falling shapes of each melody will help your child begin to experience this melodic contour in their voice.

Building Memory Skills

After a few weeks of listening and singing along, your child will be ready to begin playing the songs on the piano. They should be able to fluently sing each song in solfège (the musical language *do, re, mi,* etc.) before trying it on piano.

If your child loses the thread of the melody in the middle of the song, it can be fine to sing the next phrase for them as

> Be sure not to have the book open while playing on piano; instead, sing the song a few times with your child to rekindle their memory.

a reminder. You can also invite them to sing out loud as they play.

If your child is having a hard time remembering the songs, it is a sure sign that you need to spend more time listening to the recording and singing the songs.

Your child's young mind is constantly changing and developing. They will be deepening their mastery with each practice or listening, and even their existing knowledge needs lots of reinforcement to become permanent.

Music Notation "Pre-Reading"

The songs later in the book use traditional music notation rather than pictorial notation. This allows children to begin becoming familiar with the shapes of music notes and the five-line staff.

Please refrain from writing the solfège names over the notes of these songs. Instead, use this as an opportunity to sing the solfège words and follow along the notes. This is a valuable "pre-reading" activity and will help your child begin to notice how the notes go up and down on the lines and spaces, as well as other details of the notation.

Recitals and Special Performances

Parents' Night Out

Parents' Night Out is one idea for creating low-stakes performance opportunities during the child's early playing years.

The idea is to create a special dinner for parents, with the child providing the fancy music. Linens and candlelight are optional—take-out is fine, too! Siblings are also invited to sing or play.

For extra fun the child can set their violin case open nearby and the parents can throw coins in to show their appreciation. Children LOVE this. The dinner can be followed by a special dessert for everyone.

This event can initially begin as a celebration for when the child has learned the first twelve songs in two different keys. By now their posture should be fairly secure and they likely have some fluency on the instrument. If enjoyable, the tradition can be continued on a weekly, monthly, or occasional basis.

Parents' Night Out provides a natural incentive for the child to learn and master more repertoire, and a wonderful way for performing to feel relaxed and fun. It is a fun practice session that doesn't feel like practice for anyone!

Pop-Up Concert

This is a concert anywhere in the community. The child can invite a sibling or friend to do the concert with them! Examples:

- Someone's backyard, or the porch of an elderly neighbor
- Parent's office, during lunch or at the end of the day
- Saturday afternoon at the park or farmer's market
- During school recess or lunch, or at pick-up time for a sibling's sports, ballet, or scouting activity
- Outside the grocery store or a favorite local business
- Elementary school lobby, before a PTA meeting
- For family, either live or over Zoom (or both)
- During a church, temple, or community social event

The teacher can help your child choose the location, time, and repertoire. It may be motivating and fulfilling for your child to turn the concert into a fundraiser for their favorite charity. They can let friends and family know what they're doing and ask them to sponsor their performance.

Make sure to get a recording of your child's first pop-up concert!

Trimming Fingernails

The fingernails of the violinist's left hand must be quite short, since the pads of the fingers compress when pressing down the string. The first and second fingers meet the string at a perpendicular angle, so the edge of these nails must be well behind the fingertip.

Because young children's fingernails grow quickly, you will want to trim the left-hand fingernails daily at the beginning of practice.

Violin hand: Trim the *index and middle fingernails* as short as possible (remove all of the white). It is fine to leave a bit of white edge on the ring finger and pinky.

Bow hand: Trim the *thumb and pinky* fingernails short, so that the pads of these fingers fully contact the stick. The nails on the other fingers can be trimmed as desired.

Over time the nails of the violin hand will need to be gently trained away from the tip of the finger. Keeping the nails very short will help with this. In addition, before trimming each fingernail, clean it with the nail cleaner (even if it is not dirty), with the pointed tip tracing the bottom of the white of the fingernail. This process should feel natural and comfortable.

Training the fingernail bed away from the fingertip will provide better hand position in Book 1, and allow the student to successfully learn vibrato in Book 2.

Book 1 Graduation Recital

A book graduation recital is a rewarding way for child and family to celebrate the big accomplishment of completing Kaleidoscopes Book 1.

Your child will play a selection of the material they have learned so far. You may hold the recital in your home or at another venue such as a church or the home of a friend or relative.

This event is important for many reasons:

- Your child will feel a tremendous sense of accomplishment from playing their very own solo recital.

- Your child will be reviewing and solidifying skills learned throughout Book 1, which they will need in Book 2.

- The hard work of preparing for a recital will raise your child's skills to a higher level.

- The poise and etiquette skills used in performances require a lot of practice in order to feel natural and easy.

- Solo recitals provide a significant opportunity to become comfortable performing for others. Young children tend to be naturally far less self-conscious. Performing frequently at a young age provides a strong foundation for adolescence, when social awareness can make performing quite a bit more anxiety-provoking.

- Being the center of attention is exciting and inspiring for children (even shy children), and rewards their hard work and commitment. After experiencing their first book recital, they are typically excited when the next one arrives.

Be sure to go the extra mile to make your child's recital extra special. Treat it as you would a graduation, birthday, championship game, bar mitzvah, or other significant event. The goal is for your child to feel honored, appreciated, and excited for their accomplishments on violin.

BONUS SECTION

TOOLS FOR PARENTS

IN THIS SECTION:

Beyond Conflict: The Surprising Secret Behind Kids' Resistance and Opposition

by Deborah MacNamara, PhD

[Because Kaleidoscopes is a gentle and child-centered approach, children often genuinely love practicing … but every family experiences challenges sometimes. This article is provided here as a reference for parents both inside and outside of the practice room.]

Why is it that young children can lock down in protest at the mere suggestion of getting dressed or undressed? Why do school-age kids seem to resist directions and expectations when homework needs to get done? Why do some teens oppose and rail against rules and limits around technology use, driving them to push back at parents? At first glance, these scenarios seem unrelated … except for their capacity to ignite parental frustration and persistence. But they all share similar roots.

Kids come with an instinct to resist and oppose, or do the opposite of, what they are told. But this isn't news to parents or teachers. What may be surprising is that resistance can stem from the counterwill instinct that is innate to all humans.

The term 'counterwill' was first coined in the German language by Otto Rank, a Viennese psychoanalyst and student of Freud's. This construct was further developed by Dr. Gordon Neufeld, using the lenses of attachment and development.

Counterwill refers to the instinct to resist, counter, and oppose when feeling controlled or coerced. You can feel it arise inside of you when someone tells you what to think, do, or feel. This isn't a mistake or a flaw in human nature, and, like all instincts, serves an important function. The challenge for parents is that immaturity makes a child more prone to expressions of resistance.

Counterwill is an innate response designed to protect the self when feeling coerced or when facing separation. Children are designed to be directed by people they are attached to – which makes them prone to resist people who they are not connected to. If a stranger starts to tell a child what to do, they should be resistant to their directions. Not just anyone was meant to 'boss' a child around. This is a good thing, and preserves a parent's natural place in a child's life as being the one to care for them.

> Counterwill refers to the instinct to resist, counter, and oppose when feeling controlled or coerced.

But why do kids resist parents they are attached to? The answer is because our *have-to's* have become greater than the child's *want-to's*. In other words, their instinct to resist has become greater than their desire to follow — which could be due to the amount of control or coercion that they are experiencing, a reflection of the depth of their attachment to a parent, or their level of immaturity. A child's resistance doesn't mean we have to abandon our agenda, but it does mean we will need to figure out how to hold on to our relationship while steering through the counterwill impasse.

The counterwill instinct is also important in helping pave the way for separate functioning and becoming a unique self. Part of figuring out who you are involves placing a moratorium on other people's views, agendas, wants, and wishes. When other people's voices are louder than your own, the counterwill instinct helps to create some space through resistance so that you can develop your own perspective. While it may be problematic for parents to be resisted, it can serve an important developmental role in helping a child develop their own mind.

> The counterwill instinct helps to create some space through resistance so that you can develop your own perspective.

Counterwill responses in kids are not confined to the home and occur with other adults like teachers. The younger and more immature a child is, the more important a working relationship with their teacher will be in order to learn from them. Attachment is what opens a child's ears to real and lasting influence — not coercion, bribes, threats, rewards, or punishment.

The more responsible a parent feels to lead a child and to care for them, the more provocative acts of resistance and defiance can seem. It is sometimes challenging for parents not to react out of their own counterwill instinct when their children are locked into resistance.

What is true is that the more you push a child who is resistant, the more likely they are to push back and exhibit greater opposition. This can lead to an escalation of tension and conflict that erodes your relationship — ironically exactly what is required to render resistance less prevalent in the first place. Constant battles can create insecurity and anxiety in kids and can adversely impact their development.

The challenge is to anticipate resistance and not to take it personally. The challenge is to remain in the caretaker position and lead through the counterwill storm. Some of the strategies below require maturity in the parent and the capacity to see the big picture. It is relationship that opens a child's heart to being influenced by us and serves to create the ideal conditions for development.

So what are you supposed to do when your young child refuses to get dressed, or when your adolescent refuses to do homework or obey technology rules?

FOCUS ON CONNECTION FIRST.

What makes a child amenable to following a parent is connection. Before we direct them, we need to get into relationship by collecting them — that is, catching their eyes, getting a smile, focusing on what they are attending to — all before proceeding with our requests. If we need to talk about something that isn't working, like homework time, then it is best to collect them first to make them open to influence.

REDUCE COERCION WHEN DIRECTING.

Sometimes, when we make requests of our kids, we are talking in a coercive manner to counter their resistance before it begins. Statements like, "You have to …" or "You must …" or "You need to …" all serve to raise the counterwill instinct. Consequences are also commonly used to get a child to comply, with statements such as, "You need to do this, or else," which only exacerbates a child's resistance.

PRESS PAUSE, SIDE-STEP, AND REVISIT THE ISSUE WHEN IN BETTER ATTACHMENT.

If you are locked into a counterwill battle with a child, then it is often better to take a tactical retreat to prevent wounding

> It is sometimes challenging for parents not to react out of their own counterwill instinct when their children are locked into resistance.

to the relationship and to avoid using force to get a child to capitulate to your demands. It is also important to maintain an alpha position in doing so. For example, "I'm going to give you some time to think about this and I will be back to talk," or "I've decided this is not a good time to address this issue."

MAKE ROOM FOR THEIR OWN IDEAS AND INITIATIVE.

If a child is old enough to get dressed or organize their homework, then perhaps it is time to put them in charge of these things. If they are eager to have their own mind and exert their own wishes and wants, then carving out some spaces and turning over age-appropriate tasks to them may be a helpful strategy. The types of activities that you would not want to turn over to them would include anything to do with their caretaking such as food, or who they spend time with.

MAKE AMENDS WHEN NEEDED.

If our reactions to a child's counterwill have created distance in the relationship, then giving it time and returning to the child to make amends may be necessary. It can be simply done with an apology and an indication that you wish things would have gone better in the discussion.

While our children may claim, "You're not the boss of me," we don't have to take it to heart or react to it. We just need to lead through the counterwill storm, knowing we are their best bet and that they should feel safe and secure in our care. It is okay for our kids to have their own mind, but this doesn't mean they will always get their own way. One day the child will be the 'boss' of him or herself and until our job is done, we need to make some room for them to flex their wings, but not let go of our caretaking responsibilities.

Violin Practice: Play or Work?

While childhood is a time for delight and discovery, a healthy and balanced childhood also includes a place for discipline and responsibility. Just as children are acquiring new knowledge and physical skills, they are also developing the emotional skills that form the foundation for leading a meaningful life.

Discipline in learning a new skill should not be thought of as an undesirable restraint on a child's freedom. Rather, it is an inner quality which must be caringly taught and modeled by the parent, so that the child becomes capable of sustained effort and self-mastery.

While Kaleidoscopes is designed to make violin study enjoyable and approachable, it is not reasonable to expect that every violin practice will be a delight-filled discovery of music. The physical and mental challenge of violin means that practicing often feels like a hard work. Children (like adults!) naturally prefer easy things to hard ones.

Be frank with your child in letting them know that practicing, like going to the gym, is *work* — although of course you will both strive to make it as enjoyable as possible.

Your child will be willing to work hard because they love and respect you; when you acknowledge their work, that honors their love and effort.

> Paradoxically, it is consistent, daily practice that will allow practice time to be enjoyable and productive.

Here are some tips for ensuring a positive practice experience:

- Stay closely involved with your violin teacher; let them know immediately if you've had a difficult week. They may have helpful suggestions for you.
- Practice daily, preferably at the same time each day. The routine will come to feel natural over time.
- Choose a time of day that offers a built-in cue (e.g. after their snack). Avoid times of day that require your child to stop another activity they're immersed in.
- Limit other extra-curricular activities so your child is not overwhelmed.
- Give your child your full attention, and be positive and encouraging. This allows them to look forward to each practice and to spending quality time with you.
- Break big, hard tasks into easier, smaller ones.
- Seek out creative ways to keep things interesting. Use the practice games found at discoverviolin.org/practice-games.
- Teach your child that mental and physical work are desirable and healthy, even if they feel hard sometimes.
- Choose enjoyable activities for the beginning and end of each practice. The mind remembers beginnings and endings more strongly.
- End your practices *before* your child reaches their limit. Don't try to do "one more thing." Your child will feel more positive about practice if you end while it's still enjoyable instead of a grueling push to get everything done.
- Have a short violin practice the evening after your lesson so that you can try new assignments while both of your memories are still fresh.
- On days that your child doesn't want to practice, don't skip! Often the hardest part of practicing is simply opening the case. Just a few minutes of practice honors the commitment and preserves the routine.

Paradoxically, it is consistent, daily practice that will allow practice time to be enjoyable and productive for you and your child. Being permissive and allowing your child to skip practice will cause practice to become a source of negotiation and stormy feelings.

While eventually your child will play violin because they love it, it takes time to build the musical skill and mental endurance that allow this to happen. Meanwhile, your child needs your consistency and support. Their internal motivation will arise over time as they see the results of their efforts.

A word about vacations

Just as routines build strength and discipline, vacations rejuvenate the spirit. Once your child has been playing violin for two years or so, leaving the violin at home will be a wonderful option. Your child will appreciate your commitment to relaxation and spontaneity as much as your dedication to excellence.

However, during the first two years or so (depending on your child's age), your child's habits and skills are much more fragile. During this sensitive time, parents are advised to take the violin on most vacations.

Young children are concrete thinkers and take rules very seriously; so they will readily accept the idea of continuing to practice every day while traveling. (After all, they still have to brush their teeth, get dressed, and eat meals — why would practicing be any different?)

The practices can be quite short, but just a few minutes of playing time each day will maintain the routine, preserve the child's skills, and avoid tears and meltdowns once the family returns home.

Gentle and Wise Use of Adult Authority

Positive parenting balances respect for children with gentle yet strong adult guidance. Based in Adlerian psychology, this compassionate approach provides an alternative to both authoritarian and permissive parenting, each of which leaves certain emotional needs unmet.

An authoritarian parenting style can be described as *leadership without sensitivity*. This parent expects their orders to be obeyed quickly and without questions, and may dismiss the child's feelings or perspective.

Some children may respond to this style with submissiveness (or later, secretiveness); others may respond with defiance. Because decisions are made top-down, children's independent thinking and emotional intelligence may develop more slowly.

While authoritarian parents may have their heart in the right place (and likely see themselves as much more loving and flexible than their own parents), they may not realize how dominating they seem — especially to their child, who is physically smaller and dependent on them.

On the opposite end of the spectrum is *permissive parenting*. This can be described as *sensitivity without leadership*.

Permissiveness often comes from a desire to be compassionate, and may be a reaction to a very strict upbringing. However, too much permissiveness means no one is in charge. Instead, the household ends up being overly subject to the child's whims and impulses. Meanwhile, the lack of boundaries feels out-of-control to the child, who sees that no one is in charge (which feels scary).

The middle ground between these two styles is *authoritative parenting*, or *leadership with sensitivity*. The authoritative parent is comfortable exercising leadership and holding firm values, while also making room for their child's voice to be heard. They set clear boundaries and offer healthy choices.

Use the tools below to help you balance leadership with empathy in your own parenting.

Look for Underlying Reasons

Since children are not yet able to articulate their emotional needs, their behavior is their way of communicating with us. For example:

When Sarah becomes distractible during violin practice, she may be saying that she is worried about the new song and asking her mother to break the task into smaller steps.

When Ethan resists playing the same song over and over, he may be telling his dad that they've been doing the same thing for too long, or that he needs a game so the repetitions don't feel so grueling.

Many apparent conflicts or misbehavior are not discipline problems, but rather are simply the child communicating that something isn't working for them. In this case, focusing on the behavior simply squelches the child's feelings. A wise parent responds to the underlying need as well as the behavior itself.

> Children are more cooperative when they feel that their desires have been considered.

Offer Choices

When children feel that their desires have been considered, they are naturally more cooperative. Even if the activity itself is not optional, having some choice gives the child a sense of control.

For example, you may offer a choice about *where or when* to practice, which song to play first, or whether to focus on easier or harder activities.

Use Routines

Routines help your child to feel in control. Make sure that violin practice is at a regular time each day, and give a ten-minute reminder beforehand to help your child transition.

Catch Them Doing a Good Job

Children want to please the grown-ups in their life. When they feel they've done a good job they strive to recreate this feeling.

- Try to "catch" your child doing the desired skill; then praise their success.
- When there is a behavior you want to change, set things up so they can easily do the right behavior, then offer praise.

Build an Emotional Reservoir

Children are more cooperative when they feel loved and respected than when they feel lonely, misunderstood, or stressed. Feeling that you generally hear and respect them provides an emotional reservoir for the times when you can't give them a choice.

When your child has to do something hard, hear their feelings and let them know that you understand. Your empathy will help them to do the thing that feels challenging for them.

How to Give the Right Kind of Praise, and Avoid the Wrong Kind

While training effectively in any discipline requires rigorous attention to detail, your child must also feel free to try a new skill without worrying that they won't get it right the first time. Learning happens best in a judgment-free zone. As violin teacher Mimi Zweig says, "Mistakes are just information."

Your child needs to discover that no one is good at something when they first begin, but that hard work will pay off. This "growth mindset" is discussed in *Mindset: The New Psychology of Success*, by Carol Dweck.

The mental and emotional attitudes that comprise "growth mindset" make a bigger difference than intelligence or talent in determining who will succeed in life.

The two sources of self-esteem

The first source of a child's self-esteem is unconditional love. Your child must know that you love them for who they are and will stick with them no matter what.

The best way to communicate unconditional love is through everyday actions: being consistent and reliable, warm and caring, patient and understanding, and spending quality time with them.

The second sense of self-esteem is the self-respect that comes when your child discovers that they can accomplish meaningful things through their own work. Another name for this is *self-efficacy*.

If your child assumes that people are already just "good at" things, they will tend to reduce their efforts as soon as it seems like someone else is better than they are — even if it is an activity they enjoy.

A child who enters adult life without unconditional love will find it hard to receive affection and feel a constant need to prove themselves. A child who enters adult life without self-efficacy may enjoy fulfilling relationships, but is unlikely to achieve their personal and professional potential.

Avoid this kind of praise

Parents may offer constant praise in an effort to show unconditional love. However, this effort backfires because constant praise actually derails the second source of self-esteem. Unearned praise sends the message that your child is fragile and needs to be protected from honest feedback. Your child may internalize this as a *lack* of trust and respect. They may also come to expect constant praise and melt down in the face of real feedback from a teacher, coach, or peer. When they do receive legitimate praise, its impact is reduced because the overabundance of unearned praise has cheapened its value.

A better kind of praise

The alternative to constant praise is specific, focused praise which helps your child discover the connection between hard work and results. Some examples of this include:

- Acknowledge your child's hard work—whether or not the result was achieved.
- Acknowledge a good result and the work which led to it.
- Praise your child's actions, such as doing something the first time you ask.
- Praise your child's focus, concentration, or attitude.
- Share when their playing has moved you emotionally.

Children often have a certain outcome in mind and are frustrated when reality falls short of the mark. Rather than trying to bolster their esteem through false praise or sugarcoating, offer encouragement and help them make it better.

The friend who offers real guidance is more valuable than the friend who tells us that we're doing great when we're not.

"You're smart"

Some kinds of praise are actually detrimental to a child's self-esteem.

When a parent tells their child how smart or talented they are, this paradoxically *undermines* the child's willingness to take risks. The reason is that *the child has no control over how smart or talented they are*. They have as little control over "being" smart as they do over "being" tall.

However, once they realize that "being" smart is important to you, they will begin trying to keep your good opinion. The next time they don't understand something or make a mistake, they will worry that they're actually *not* smart. Not wanting to disappoint you, they will avoid making mistakes — which essentially means not trying anything new. The may hide when they do not understand something, or even underachieve out of an unconscious need to find out if you will still love them.

When you praise your child, make sure that it's clear how their result is connected to their *effort*, rather than to an intrinsic quality such as smartness or talent. This will encourage them to continue working hard, both because they are getting results, and because their efforts are seen and appreciated.

Encouraging and Coaching Your Child

Words and phrases to build skill, character, and confidence

GENERAL POSITIVE FEEDBACK

General feedback is not the most useful kind by itself, but helps keep the tone of practice positive.

Great job!

Good work!

Outstanding!

Wow!

Way to go!

Outstanding!

Excellent work!

A+!

Wow. That's the best you've ever played that!

Very nice.

Beautiful playing!

RESULT ATTAINED

This feedback helps your child know when they've gotten it right, while offering encouragement.

That's it!

You did it!

I knew you could do it.

YES.

Yes! You figured it out.

You got it right!

You got it on the first try!

INFORMATIVE FEEDBACK

USE THIS TYPE OF FEEDBACK MOST OFTEN!

Informative feedback provides detailed information about a specific skill. It tells your child both what went well (so they can keep doing this), and that you noticed and valued this accomplishment.

Since the affirmation portion of the feedback is indirect, this leaves room for your child to affirm himself / herself. This builds their inner compass and avoids them becoming overly reliant on external praise.

You held your violin high the whole time!

Your third finger was exactly in tune!

You had clear spaces between your staccato notes.

Your notes had beautiful feathered endings.

Your bow and fingers were moved exactly together that time.

I didn't hear a single crunchy sound!

You kept your bowhold the whole time!

ENCOURAGING FEEDBACK

In the early stages of working on a new skill, different language is needed. Honesty is a necessary quality of a good coach, and your child is counting on you to help them improve!

The phrases below provide useful feedback while still being encouraging.

That's much better! Can you do it again?

That's the best one you've done so far.

Oooh. It's really getting there!

You're on the right track.

That's a great start. Try again!

You got it! Let's do five just like that!

It's getting more consistent!

It's getting better and better!

You have the hang of it. Do a few more and let's see how good it can get!

TAKING IT TO THE NEXT LEVEL

This type of feedback helps to create the narrative that we are all learning and growing. It also creates the value of striving toward excellence.

Your notes are so clean and in tune. I think you may be ready to try going a little faster. What do you think?

Wow! Very nice. I think you are ready to think about another idea! What could we make better next?

You did such a great job playing in tune. Are you ready to work on keeping your bow straight?

APPRECIATING PERSONAL QUALITIES

This feedback is powerful and deeply affirming because it is reflecting your child's positive qualities back to them. Keep this feedback in balance with task-focused types of feedback.

I appreciate how detailed you are being!

I can tell that you want to make it really good.

I see you really working hard today.

I see how strong your body is getting!

I can tell that you really care about making a beautiful tone.

Temperament Traits of Children

Research shows that personality is determined by the interaction of temperament traits with the environment. Each person comes with "factory-installed" wiring ... e.g. the eight temperament traits listed below. These temperament traits are considered relatively stable from birth.

How a child is wired can determine how they respond to various situations ... as well as how well they "fit" with those around them. A child whose temperament fits well with their environment will be received well by those around them; they will experience interactions as positive and fulfilling.

When the child's temperament differs from that of their parents, identifying these differences can help parents to avoid frustration and tailor their expectations and parenting to match their child's unique disposition.

Practice games can help balance the activity of practicing with the child's natural temperament. For example, kinetic activities may provide an outlet for active, stimulus-seeking children; quiet, artistic activities provide a "breather" for quieter children. Both types will adapt fantasy play to their individual interests and activity level.

Activity Level	Distractibility	Adaptability	Persistence
The child's usual "idle speed" or activity level. • Do they always wiggle, squirm or fidget? • Do they have trouble sitting still? • Are they content to sit and quietly watch, or are they always on the go? • Do they prefer quiet, sedentary activities? Highly active children may channel extra energy into sports. They may perform well in high-energy careers and be able to keep up with many responsibilities.	Degree of concentration when a child is not particularly interested in an activity. • Does the child become sidetracked easily when attempting to follow routine? • How long does the child maintain focus on a low-rewarding activity? High distractibility is seen as positive when it is easy to divert a child from an un-desirable behavior; negative when it prevents the child from completing tasks.	How easily the child adapts to change — e.g. transitioning to a new activity. • Does the child have difficulty with changes in routines? • Do they resist going from one activity to another? • Do they take a long time to become comfortable in new situations? A slow-to-adapt child is less likely to rush into dangerous situations, but may also be less flexible, open-minded and spontaneous.	How long a child continues in the face of obstacles. • Does the child stay with a difficult puzzle, or do they lose interest? • Is the child able to wait to have his needs met? (A more impulsive child will be more impatient.) A persistent child is labeled "stubborn" when they persist in an activity they are asked to stop, but "patient" when they work through a tough puzzle. These children achieve goals, but may also perseverate in an unproductive direction.
Approach / Withdraw	Sensory Threshold	Intensity	Mood
The child's typical response to a new situation or person. • Does the child eagerly approach new situations or people? • Or does the child seem hesitant and resistant when faced with new situations or people? Slow-to-warm-up children tend to think before they act. They are less likely to act impulsively during adolescence.	Level of sensitivity to physical stimuli (sounds, tastes, touch, temperature changes). • Does the child react positively or negatively to particular sounds? • Do they startle easily? • Do they respond positively or negatively to the feel of clothing? Highly sensitive individuals are more likely to be artistic & creative. Less sensitive children may seek stronger sensory stimulation.	Energy level of a response — whether positive or negative. • Does the child react strongly to everything — even minor events? • Does the child show emotions strongly and dramatically? • Or does the child just get quiet when upset? Intense children experience *all* emotions more intensely. They may be creative and artistic. Intense children may be exhausting sometimes.	The tendency to react to the world primarily in a positive or negative way. • Does the child tend to focus on the positive or negative aspects of situations? • Is the child generally in a happy mood? • Is the child generally serious? Serious children may be hard on themselves and others, but they also tend to be analytical and thoughtful.

Children perceived as "more difficult" tend to be *high in* activity, distractibility, intensity, sensitivity, and withdrawal; *low* in adaptability and persistence; and more negative in mood.

Practice Games: Making Practice Delightful for Your Young Child

Practice games are only one of many tools you will need to ensure the quality and regularity of home practice.

First, though, a reminder.

As parents, our words and actions must communicate, "Practicing violin is important and hard work. Even if it's not fun, it's still required"— rather than, "Practicing should be fun. If it's hard work or emotionally challenging, we don't have to do it."

> Often the right practice game will yield better results than a stern attitude.

We are looking to balance two important goals. First, we want our child to strive toward their fullest potential. We want them to have a strong mind and a strong body, and to achieve excellence in their chosen art. This requires hard work and daily discipline.

And ... we want their violin playing to be a source of lifelong pleasure. We want them to think of their violin with love and not as a burden — although of course we know practicing may feel hard from time to time. We want the time we spend together to be productive, but also positive.

How Do We Balance Those Two Goals?

Be serious, but also be playful. *These qualities are natural complements, not opposites.* In the workplace or research lab the most creative and productive teams are those characterized by humor, affection, and play.

Be committed to excellence but not attached to when things are mastered. Master tiny details, but always inside a commitment to joyful work. Quality time will yield excellent results over time. Every child has a different path.

Practice games are more powerful than they may appear. Often the right practice game will yield better results than a stern attitude. Practice game fill the gap when a given activity isn't yet intrinsically rewarding.

Goals of Practice Games

- To empower your child's innate capacity for hard work
- To make concrete a process whose rewards are long-term and not readily perceived or understood by a young child
- To provide variety to the practice, allowing the child to sustain their efforts for a longer period of time
- To encourage the child to bring their own creativity to the practice
- To enrich violin practice through imaginative journeys and dialogue which extend beyond violin practice, expanding the relationship between parent and child
- To create an experience of discovery and joy in violin practice

Practice Game Examples

DECORATING TREE

Find an inexpensive jewelry tree. Gather a collection of child-friendly wine-glass charms or earrings. These may also be made from beads and colored wire. For every 3–4 repetitions the child may hang 1 charm on the tree.

PRACTICE JAR

Decorate a juice jar with a violin and child's name. For each 10 or 15 minutes of good practice, place one bead in the jar. When the glass is full they get a prize (chosen in advance), such as choosing a new book, trip to a children's museum, finger painting, choosing Friday's dinner menu, etc.

INCHES AND YARDS

Find a yardstick and a brightly colored binder clip. For every repetition, the child gets to move the binder clip down the ruler. Small children enjoy watching the number get higher and higher ... and reach the end and go the other way!

STEP-BY-STEP ARTWORK

Gather some enticing beads and coated string. For each 3–5 repetitions the child may choose one bead. When they acquire a certain number, they can string them on the bracelet at the end of practice. 5–6 practices complete a whole bracelet. A coloring page can be used in a similar way.

DECORATE HOUSE

The student may place one furnishing in a doll-house every 4 repetitions. (Young boys love this as much as girls!)

RIBBON HIDE-AND-SEEK

For very young children. Gather 5-6 colorful gift bows & hide them around the room. For each 3-5 repetitions the child may find one bow.

Visit discoverviolin.org/practice-games to find many ideas to create practices that are as enjoyable for you as they are for your child. Use these ideas to create your set of games that are unique to your child's temperament and interests!

Siblings in the Practice Room

While it might be ideal for you to sit down and give your child undivided time, sometimes a younger sibling may simply need attention, and it's just you.

If this is the case, here are some creative ways can you find to practice with your child, while still meeting the needs of the younger sibling.

- Find a special activity for the younger sibling that can be reserved just for music practice, which they can continue to do as long as they stay quiet. A simple game such as Candyland™ can also work.

- Engage the younger sibling in "helping" their older sister / brother ... for example, by watching their bowhold, making sure their violin stays lifted, or placing a pebble in a jar for each time they play a song.

- Find a (moderately) quiet physical activity that you can participate in with the younger sibling, while your visual attention is still on the child who is practicing. For example, rolling a ball back and forth, helping them walk a balance beam, or playing hide and seek with a small object.

There may not always be a perfect solution, but whatever steps you can take toward being fully involved in your child's practice will help them to succeed in learning new skills, feel a sense of support and companionship, and progress on their instrument in a way that feels satisfying.

The Importance of Singing

As your child begins violin lessons, it is very easy to treat the songs as a medium for learning "the important thing" — playing the violin (a.k.a. the thing you're spending money on).

However, this would be a huge missed opportunity!

Practical Reasons to Sing

As your child begins Kaleidoscopes, you should sing the songs with your child as you go about your day.

Singing the songs frequently will help your child internalize them more deeply. As they gain mastery of the song, they will feel excited to begin it on violin, and will learn it more quickly, which will further increase their confidence and excitement.

On a more fundamental musical level, singing will help your child to develop their pitch, rhythm, phrasing, and vocal control. Having a repertoire of well-known songs will develop their aural awareness — which is especially important for violin. The fingerboard does not have frets so violinists must find notes by *hearing* them mentally.

And, of course, singing supports language development, attention, working memory, and reading ability.

Our Personal Instrument

As important as all of these skills may be, several emotional aspects of singing are equally important.

Singing is your child's first instrument. It will be take a long time for their instrumental proficiency to catch up to their singing; so singing will continue to be their most fluent musical expression for quite some time.

Having a secure relationship to one's own voice is important, because singing is one of the most personal means of musical expression. The physicality of making a powerful vocal sound challenges us to express ourselves boldly, building trust in our voice and our ideas. The vibration in our jaw and facial bones stimulates the vagus nerve, which regulates our heart rate and brings a physical sense of calm and relaxation. The vibration of singing resonates in every cell of our body, energizing our nervous system and allowing emotions to flow more freely.

As children develop social awareness, social pressures may cause them to become shy about their own singing. For example, if their vocal control is less proficient and they are matching pitch less accurately than their peers, they may notice that they are out of tune and lose confidence. Or they may judge themselves for not sounding like pop stars they hear on recordings, not realizing that these artists have had years of tWraining.

This process is something many of us adults have also experienced ... and may need to overcome in order to tap into the joy of singing with our child.

Creating Community Through Song

Singing with your child bridges the gap between practice room and family room. Family music-making will strengthen your bond with your child and foster a sense of belonging. All family members can participate in musical expression through singing, which can be an important cornerstone of family life.

Shared songs are also a thread which connects us to previous generations. Your child will remember and cherish the songs they shared with you, and share them with their own children.

Create a Family Culture of Music-Making

Creating a musical family isn't about "training." It happens when you find ways to make music as you go through the day.

- Choose a bright, affectionate song to wake your child in the morning.
- For younger children, find enjoyable songs for changing diapers, bouncing, and finger play.
- Take familiar songs and change the words to match any occasion — washing the dishes, folding laundry, or getting ready in the morning. This makes chores fun!
- Make a playlist for cleaning
- Make a dancing playlist for after dinner!

- Sing while waiting in line at the grocery store, driving to school, or getting stuck in traffic.
- Rock out in the car! Drum on the steering wheel while your child claps, shakes a cracker box, etc.

Your family will be a more joyful place when music expands beyond the practice room. Enjoy the process of discovering your musical creativity in this safe haven you and your significant other are creating together.

An Introduction to Guided Discovery

Kaleidoscopes blends the Suzuki approach of detailed parental guidance with the Montessori idea of fostering the child's own self-teaching. How can these two seemingly opposite approaches be brought together?

Developing correct violin posture requires a high level of perfect practice. Once bad habits are formed, correcting them can be nearly impossible. For this reason, your detailed help is essential. You don't want your child to learn posture through guided discovery — they'll just end up with bad posture.

However, in areas other than posture, there are many opportunities to foster your child's choice, independence and exploration. Here are some examples:

> *"As you play Twinkle, what posture point would you like to focus on first?"*
>
> *"Let's choose one 'safe and easy' song and one 'little bit hard' song to practice today."*
>
> *"You've never played that note before! How exciting! I'm not sure where it is either. Let's try different ones and see which one sounds right."*

In this last instance, perhaps you actually remember where the unfamiliar note is (but your child has forgotten). It would be so easy to tell your child where the note is! Or perhaps you don't know, and are tempted to simply ask the teacher.

Simply providing the answer isn't the best learning, though. It's more powerful to let your child find it for themselves. They'll get it eventually, and the mistakes along the way are discoveries in their own right.

When you give your child room to work through a problem on their own, they will learn that they can figure things out for themselves. The process of effortful engagement will sharpen their problem-solving skills and scientific thinking.

> When you give your child room to work through a problem on their own, they will learn that they can figure things out for themselves.

As their discernment grows, they will be able to handle open-ended problems and greater complexity, gradually building the cognitive sophistication required for full independence. This builds confidence and perseverance.

It's fine to offer a little help — in fact, they will need this! But *guide* them toward the answer, rather than simply handing them the answer key.

But Isn't It Faster to Give Them the Answer?

There are many good reasons that teachers and parents may be tempted to "help" a child too much:

- We can remember when our child was very young and needed our help for *everything*. As they grow up, our image of them may lag behind; we may assume they are more dependent than they are.
- Offering help is a natural, empathetic response. We know what it feels like to need help and we naturally provide this.
- We may feel anxious when we see our child experience frustration.
- We may take the words, "I need help" literally, rather than as a request for encouragement or support.
- Spending most of our lives in the workplace as competent and results-oriented adults, it may be hard for us to tolerate inefficiency and errors.
- Many of us were taught in a more didactic way, so our teaching instincts naturally lean this direction.

The guided discovery process may take a bit longer, and sometimes it may be hard to be patient. However, when you let your child be the "lead investigator," it sends the message that you trust their intelligence and resourcefulness. In turn, they develop confidence and learn to trust themselves.

CHAPTER 2

EARNING THE VIOLIN & BOW

If your child is age 3–5, they will not receive their violin right away. Instead, they will first develop some musical and postural skills that will set them up for success on the instrument.

This section will be a valuable reference to you as their home practice coach.

(FOR YOUNG BEGINNERS)

IN THIS SECTION:

Earning the Violin

For a young child (age 3–5), playing the violin presents significant challenges:

- Elevating and twisting their left arm sideways while holding their right arm at chest level;

- Maintaining this twisted position while supporting a wooden box in an elevated position, seemingly for eternity;

- Manipulating each of the fingers independently and in an exact sequence, in view of only the left eye;

- Keeping the wrist (which is hidden under the violin) in the correct, straight position while pressing their fingers downward, supported only by a previously anonymous bone in their thumb; and

- Pulling a stick at a consistent angle, oblique to the body, on a string which is separated from adjacent strings by an angle of only 10°.

For this reason, young beginners do not start immediately on the violin, but instead learn movement activities which will help these difficult motions to feel natural in their bodies.

At the same time as they are practicing these Movement Building Blocks, they will be learning several songs on piano. On piano, they can easily play in tune and with a beautiful tone, providing them with the immediate success that every young child desires. Over just a few weeks' time they will be able to play many songs, giving them a sense of mastery and confidence.

As your child discovers each song on the piano, they will learn how to associate each finger with its own note. Their hands will develop strength and they will develop an awareness of the individual fingers.

> Learning the songs on piano will help your child begin to understand the relationships of the notes in their songs.

They will also begin to understand the relationships of the notes in their songs — for example, which notes are higher and lower, which notes are adjacent, and which notes are a "skip" away.

Once they have graduated the required piano songs and Movement Building Blocks, your child will have earned their violin! This is an exciting day, and the long sought-after violin is an amazing reward for their hard work. They will feel very proud of their accomplishment, and rightfully so. They will also be very motivated to begin the next chapter in their study — playing on the violin itself!

The next step is learning to finger the violin *while seated on the floor with the violin in front of them*. In this position they can easily see their fingers; which for young children is necessary in order to move the correct one. Placing the violin on the left shoulder before they are ready can be difficult and confusing; they will tend to move the violin in front of them for better visibility, which may become a bad habit.

The fluency they attain while playing the violin in "cello position" will accelerate their progress when they are ready to begin playing violin in "shoulder position." They will have already developed muscle memory for the movements of fingering, and can focus on the most difficult aspect of playing — managing the movement of the bow and coordinating the bow and fingers.

Materials Needed During This Early Stage

Piano or keyboard

For the first few months the child will be learning songs on the piano. If possible, invest in an instrument with weighted keys (so it feels similar to a real piano and builds finger strength), touch sensitivity, and a minimum of 76 keys.

Although a neighbor's or relative's piano will be enjoyable to explore, it is best to have an instrument in your own home so that your child can practice anytime they wish. Your child will love the songs and will often go to the piano and play simply for the joy of making music.

Small items for manipulatives

Some of the Movement Building Blocks involve manipulatives to develop manual dexterity and finger independence. Small objects such as pom-poms, jacks, dice, or rubber miniatures make good manipulatives that are easy enough to pick up and also interesting from both a visual and tactile perspective.

Ideally, these items should be reserved for violin practice. This makes them "special" and will increase the enjoyment of practicing.

Open the back of your child's Kaleidoscopes book to view the "Earn Your Violin" page.
Your child will work through these activities during their first 6–12 months of study.

Learning the Songs Using Solfège

Solfège is the name of the musical language used to name the notes of the scale — *do, re, mi, fa, so, la, ti,* and *do.*

The advantage of the movable-do system is its ease of singing and ability to move fluidly from key to key. It is best to save alphabetic note names until a bit later, to avoid confusion.

The first step for your child to begin mastering their songs is to sing them with you as well as with the recording. Sing with your child as much as possible, and set your daily activities to music!

In most cases the solfège will actually be easier for your child to remember than the lyrics. However, be sure to practice both.

> Practice singing the songs while keeping a steady beat, alternating lap taps with fingertip touches. Avoid loud movements such as clapping, which cover up the music.

Encourage your child to use their singing ("light" or "soft") voice rather than their speaking ("heavy") voice.

During home practice, sit on the floor together and keep a steady beat to the songs. Use your body to show strong and weak beat — e.g. pat your lap, then touch your fingertips together. This will help them to develop a sense of pulse, which is the foundation of good rhythm.

Avoid clapping, which covers up the music.

Also practice singing the songs while pointing at each note on the pictorial song notation. This will help your child learn to follow the notes from left to right.

Learning the Songs on Piano

Playing piano will be used as a stepping-stone to help internalize the songs and build finger awareness before moving to violin.

While many parents may have begun their own piano studies in C major, this curriculum begins in D major for the following reasons:

1. A child who does not yet know left and right can find *do* much more easily in D major, since *do* is located *between* the two black keys.

2. The hand position is more natural, with the tallest finger being on a black key.

3. It is the easiest key for children to sing.

4. The violinists in group class can easily play in this key.

5. It introduces the two most common sharps used in violin playing — and in a visually clear and tactile way.

1. One-Finger Playing

When playing piano for the first time, a very young child will probably use just their index finger to play each note. This feels easy and natural for them, and they are welcome to continue doing this until they have the attention and coordination to move to independent fingering. The younger the child, the longer this will take.

Use books to raise the seat to the correct height, and place a stool under your child's feet for support.

"Giraffes and Elephants" (black key groups of 2 and 3 notes) is the perfect exercise to introduce adjacent fingers. This will build finger independence, which can then be transferred to Hot Cross Buns and other songs when the child is ready.

Your child may choose to play Hot Cross Buns for a long time before moving to the next song. That is fine! Let them enjoy their success on this easy song. They will venture to the next song when they are ready.

In general, the songs can be played in any order; the song your child chooses is likely the song they are ready for.

2. Independent Fingers, Hands Separate

When your child is ready, introduce the idea that each finger has its own note ("*mi-re-do* fingers"). When playing with the right hand, the thumb is *do*. Keep the wrist lifted and the fingertips on the keys, maintaining a curved shape.

When your child is ready for a new challenge, they can learn to play their easiest songs with their left hand. Now *do* is played by the pinky. Practice songs with each hand separately.

3. Copy-Hands (Hands Parallel)

Last, combine hands together. Although initially difficult to coordinate, even a very young child can be successful in a few days when they have mastered the previous steps. This will be a big victory for them!

Most songs use the notes *do–so*, which fits comfortably in a five-finger span. For songs which use notes outside this range, allow the child to find these note in whatever way is most natural for them. More sophisticated fingerings can be introduced later, when the child is ready for a new skill.

In cello position the right thumb rests against the edge of the fingerboard.

Playing Violin in "Cello Position"

Since this position is a temporary one, the teacher can focus on fingering skills while postponing posture challenges for a little while.

Children 3–5 years old begin by plucking the violin in cello position, since at this age they have a strong need to see their fingers in order to isolate the correct movement. Cello position allows them to be comfortable while they build the coordination to lift and place each finger, as well as building finger strength.

For the left (fingering) hand shape, think "C for cello." When they begin playing with the violin on the shoulder, the hand shape will be "V for violin."

The fingers can be placed independently or additively — whichever is more comfortable. Each finger is placed on its corresponding tape.

Initially the parent will pluck. When the child is ready to pluck, their right thumb should rest against the bottom edge of the fingerboard.

Practice Guidelines During the "Earn Your Violin" Phase

With most children, parents should do two practices each day: a "review" practice (playing familiar songs a few times each), and a second practice which focuses on new songs and movement building blocks.

During the review portion, have your child play *each song* they know, 2–3 times each ... so they are playing every song in their repertoire, every day. Their fluency on these songs will get deeper and deeper over time.

For their newer songs, a rule of thumb is to repeat items the same number as their current age — so if they are four years old, do four repetitions.

Always move to a new activity when your child's attention begins to wane. This will help keep practice enjoyable. Their attention span will lengthen naturally with practice and maturity.

Begin each practice on an easy, enjoyable activity. Now introduce a more challenging activity, while your child's attention is still fresh. Continue alternating easy and challenging activities throughout the practice.

When you see your child beginning to tire, it's time to end the practice. Choose a fun activity for this. The last activity is how your child will remember the whole practice session, so be sure to end on a high note!

VIOLIN MOVEMENT BUILDING BLOCKS

used for young students to "earn" their violin

In addition to the skills noted on each exercise below, all of these activities reinforce moving to the beat of the song. All movements should be performed to the quarter note beat. Parents can find child-friendly videos at discoverviolin.org.

Hot Cross Buns: Tray of Cookies

Movement from the elbow; awareness of arm level

1. Lift both arms straight out at shoulder level.
2. Bend the *right* forearm from the elbow so the fingertips touch the inside of the left elbow.
3. Return to the original position.
4. Do this to the beat, keeping both arms level and lifted.

Added challenge: Balance an eraser on the right hand.

Let Us Chase the Squirrel: Nuts in the Backpack

Shoulder strength; midline crossing; bow path

1. Extend the left arm out straight, palm up.
2. Place a "nut" in the palm (any small object).
3. Use the right hand to move the "nut" from the left hand to the left shoulder, tracing a large arc through the air.

Continue alternating the object from palm to shoulder, making sure the left arm stays elevated. Do this motion to the beat.

Boil Them Cabbage: Bunny Hops

Preparing the bow hand; right shoulder strength; midline crossing

1. Make a "bow bunny" with the right hand by placing the pads of the middle fingers against the thumbnail.
1. The bunny nods "yes" and "no." *Do you like eating carrots? How about spaghetti?*
2. Place the bunny on the opposite shoulder. The bunny hops up and down to the beat of the song. Get the bounces as high as possible to build strength in the right shoulder.

Do this with just the hand. Later, do it with a pencil ("carrot") placed between the fingers and thumb.

Children find this exercise moderately strenuous. It also develops muscle memory for playing at the frog.

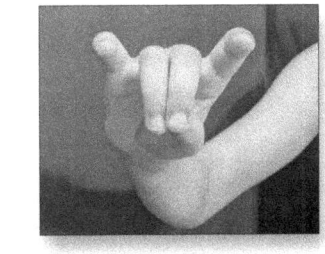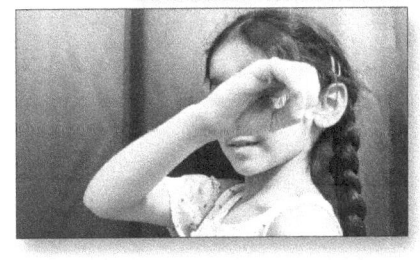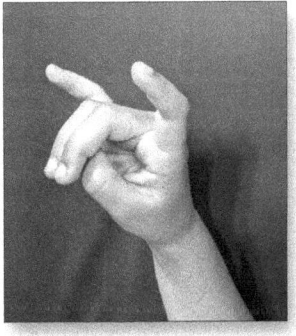

All My Little Ducklings: Duck Wings *Shoulder strength; elbow rotation; body awareness*

Follow the 4-beat pattern: "Square, elbows, square, wings," as outlined below:

With hands and wrists flat, form both arms into square corners ("strong arm" position).

Touch both elbows together at the midline.

Return to the original position.

Open the bent arms wide ("spread your wings").

Bingo: Doggy Perks His Ears *Establishing independence of the index and pinky*

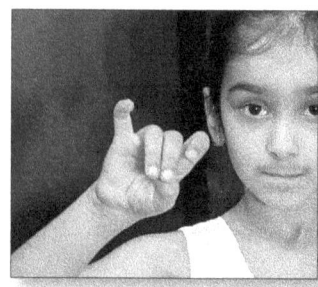 

Make a bow bunny. Alternate raising the pinky and the index finger to the beat of the song.

All Around the Buttercup: Bunny in the Meadow *Maintaining the bow hand in the presence of distraction*

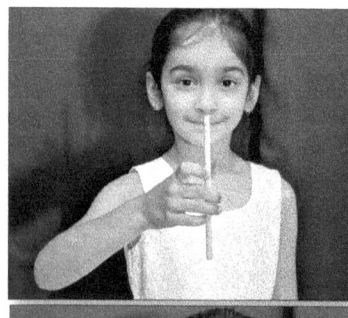

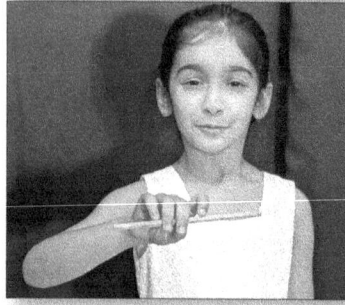

For this exercise, use a "bow bunny" without a pencil, or half-bowhold (index and pinky on top, as pictured to the left). Sing the song using the motions below. Notice that as the notes go up ("one, two, three") the pencil raises; as they go down, it lowers.

"All around the buttercup	Hold the pencil vertically; trace horizontal circles.
... one	... turn the pencil horizontal
... two	... raise the pencil
... three"	... raise the pencil
"If you want a bonny lass	Turn the pencil upright and draw circles as before.
... just	... turn the pencil horizontal
... choose	... lower the pencil
... me."	... lower the pencil

As a more advanced option, do the first several steps of the bowhold on a pencil and perform the song with the bowhold (or proto-bowhold).

Birds' Wedding: Birds' Nest & Birds' Eggs

Individuating and strengthening the fingers of the left hand

Verses 1-4: Strongly tap each finger of the *left* hand to the thumb — one finger for each verse.

Verse 5: Tap the pinky of the *right* hand to the thumb.

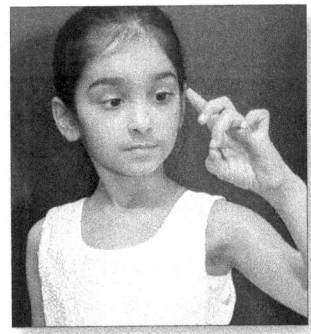

Verse 6: Match the fingers of both hands together to create a round birds' nest. Alternately press and release while maintaining the "nest" shape. *The child can observe the end of the finger turn slightly white when pressing, and pink upon release.*

Reuben & Rachel: Teasing Friends

Keeping the index of the bow hand released while the thumb bends

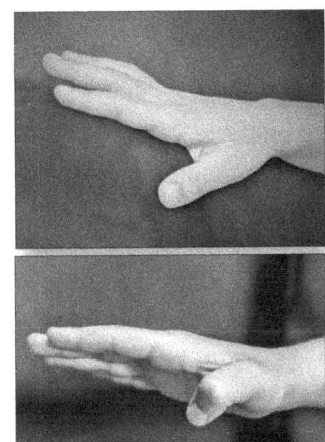

Begin with the right hand open and flat.

Bend and open the thumb to the beat, keeping the other fingers straight.

Paw Paw Patch: Bending Down for a Paw Paw

Keeping the thumb of the violin hand straight while the index bends

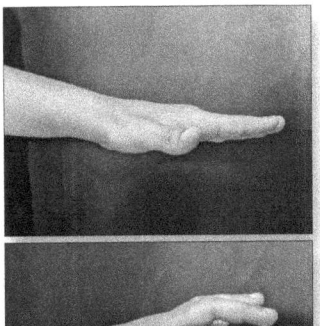
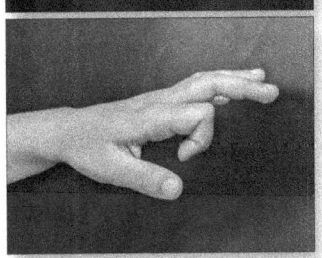

Begin with the left hand open and flat.

Bend and open the index finger to the beat, keeping the thumb straight and relaxed. *It is normal for the remaining fingers to bend slightly.*

Mary Had a Little Lamb: Nose to Tail *Rotation of the left arm and hand; curved hand shape*

In Front of the Body

Get ready by locating the pinky and curving it. Practice looking through the pinky curve at various objects in the room.

1. Begin with the left arm dropped at the side, head forward.
2. Touch the *side* of the curved left pinky to the tip of the nose. This is the "nose-to-tail" position.
3. Drop the arm.

Perform this to a 2-beat pattern: "Down, nose, down, nose."

Add the Head-Turn

Warm up by practicing turning the nose to the left (violin) shoulder. Only the head should turn; the body should still face forward.

Again perform the steps above, this time with the "nose-to-tail" position on the left violin side of the body (as pictured).

Four-Step Version *(not pictured)*

1. Start with the arm at the side and head looking forward.
2. Simultaneously turn the head and touch the pinky to the nose.
3. Extend the arm to violin playing position.
4. Bring the pinky back to the nose.

Follow the 4-beat pattern: "Down, nose, extend, nose."

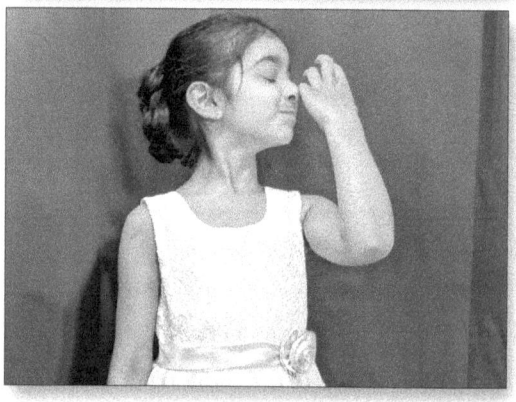

This Old Man: Banana & Scissors *Ability to individually adjust the lateral spacing of the fingers*

Young students are still developing control of the interosseus muscles. Located in the palm of the hand, these muscles spread the fingers and press them together. Without individual control of the fingers in this lateral dimension, students' bowing and fingering hands may end up either all bunched together or all spread out.

Do the following activities with each hand, *but just one hand at a time*, to the beat of the song:

- First, have the child open and close just a single finger — first the pinky alone, then the index alone.
- The "helper hand" can hold two fingers stationary while the others move. This helps the child isolate the target muscles.
- Keeping the hand relaxed makes it easier. Help the child to discover the minimal exertion needed to hold the desired fingers together.
- Placing the hand on a table can also help; the non-moving fingers can press into the table.
- Finally, do the full actions pictured to the right.

Transformation Challenge

Turn your scissors into a banana and back, following a four-beat pattern: Banana, Scissors, Banana, Scissors.

Peel the Banana

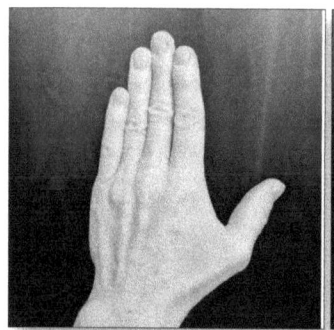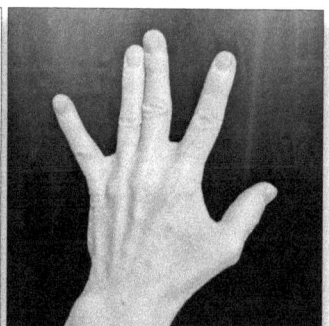

Scissors

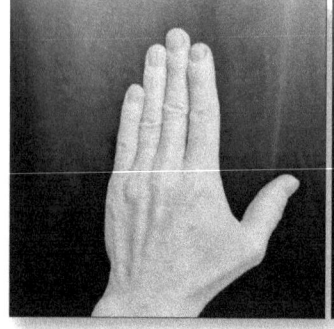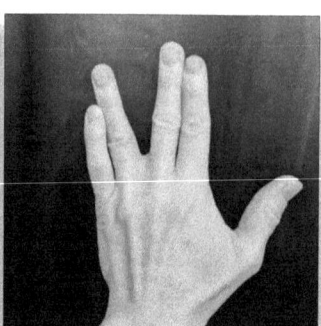

Yankee Doodle: Finger Soldiers

Left-hand technique: The first finger square, separating index from the other fingers; aligning the index with the hand

"Yankee Doodle went to town..."

Close the fingertips into squares. Keep the thumb straight.

Extend the fingers, allowing the spacing to expand.

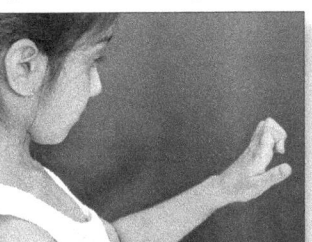 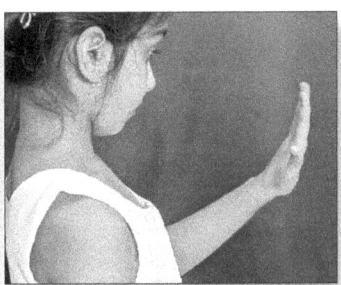

Keep the base joints aligned with the hand—don't tilt them into the palm. (The soldiers don't want to fall into the mud.) The wrist & thumb should be relaxed and straight.

"Yankee Doodle, keep it up..." (refrain)

Hold the first finger in a square; wiggle the other fingers and thumb.

Keep the index finger aligned with the back of the hand. This is the captain — he is in charge of the soldiers cleaning the camp.

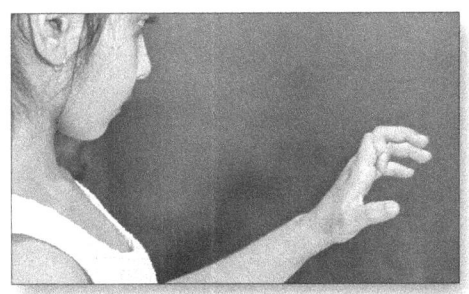

Skip to My Lou: Bows & Bumps

Movement from the elbow versus the shoulder

Form a bow bunny with the hand. Start with the arm squared, then follow the pattern, "Bow, square, bump, square":

 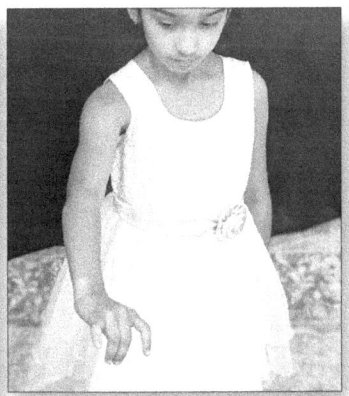 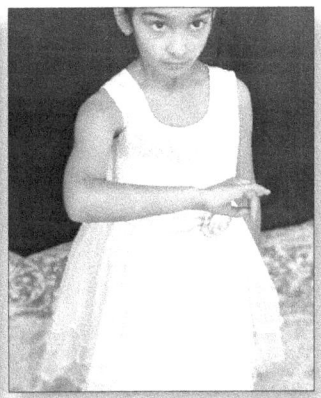 

Bend the arm into a square at chest level.

Open the forearm from the elbow ("open the gate"). The wrist should bend. *This is the correct motion for bowing.*

Return the arm to a square ("close the gate").

"Freeze" the square and open the entire arm from the shoulder. *Don't rotate the trunk of the body; only the arm should move.*

Twinkle Twinkle: Stargazing Pinky

Extension of the bow pinky; independence of the pinky

Make a bow bunny on the pencil. The pinky should be curved.

Stabilize the pencil with the helper hand. Extend the pinky, sliding it along the ring finger. *The pinky is gazing up at the night sky.*

Return the pinky to a curved position on the pencil.

Perform the motion to a two-beat pattern while singing. Make sure the index finger stays curved while the pinky extends.

This is a preparation for "Flapping the Wings" (in the "Earn Your Bow" sequence).

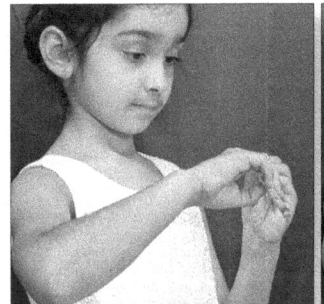 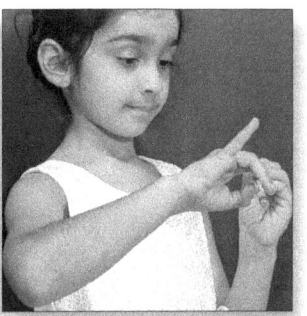

Naughty Kitty: Knuckle Awareness   *Control of angle of the base joints (violin- and bow-hand skill)*

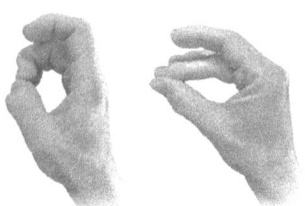

 Eggs & Alligators

This knuckle awareness experience helps students understand the inverse relationship between the angle of the knuckles and the curve of the fingers.

Touch the tips of the middle finger and thumb together, on the bow hand (the "egg"). The knuckles will be fairly flat. Now move to an "alligator" shape (extended fingers). The kunckles are quite angled in this shape. Observe this relationship with interest.

 Soft Paws, Swat the Dog *(a friendly reminder who's boss)*    **The Claws Come Out** *(doggy needs a lesson)*

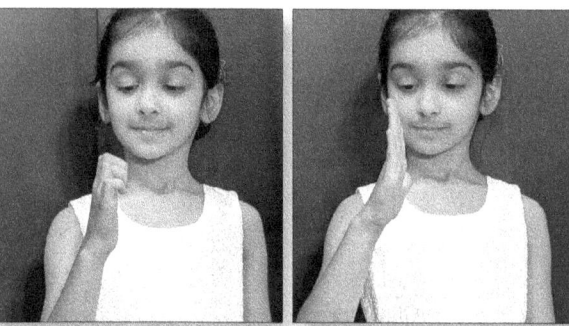   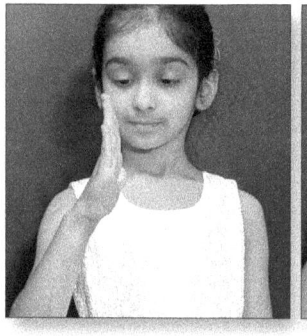 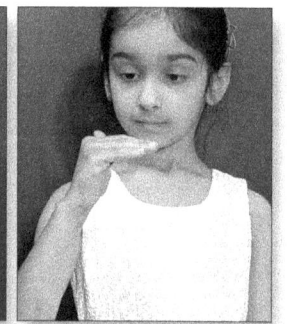

Practice exercises ② and ③ above in a two-beat pattern, with both left and right hands (one hand at a time).

 Kitty Jiu Jitsu: After mastering ② and ③ above, kitty is ready for the "black belt" paw training! Combine the motions into a four-beat pattern: "Soft paws, swat, soft paws, claws."

White Coral Bells: Fairy Ballet   *Discovering the angle of the hand and forearm (playing at the frog and tip)*

Follow the 4-beat pattern: "Straight, down, straight, up," as outlined below. When ready, combine the individual movements into a continuous, fluid motion.

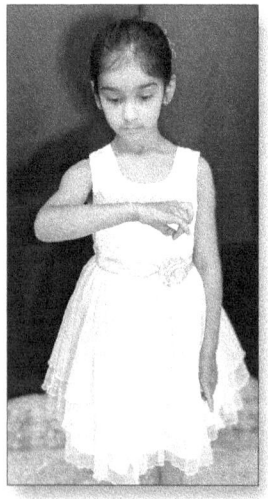 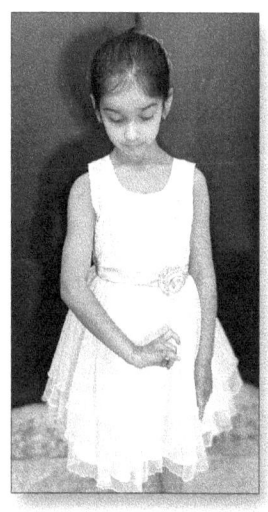  

Make a bow bunny. Hold the hand horizontally at chest level, elbow bent.

Lower to the waist, keeping the hand level. The wrist will make a concave angle.

Notice the elbow is above the hand. This is like playing at the tip.

Return to the original position.

Raise above the head, keeping the hand level. The wrist will make a convex angle.

Now the hand is above the elbow. This is like playing at the frog.

Love Somebody: Silent Violin & Bow *Differentiation of the roles of the left and right arms*

Two-Step Silent Violin

Begin with both arms dropped.

Rotate the left arm into violin position, while simultaneously raising the bow arm into a square. The bow hand should form a "bow bunny."

Perform the "Down-up" motion to a two-beat pattern while singing the song.

Four-Step Silent Violin

Do the first two steps above, then add a bowing motion ("open the gate, close the gate"). The movement is now "Drop, ready, open, close."

Make sure both wrists are straight, the left fingers are lifted and curved, the bow arm is level with the chest, and the bow arm opens from the elbow.

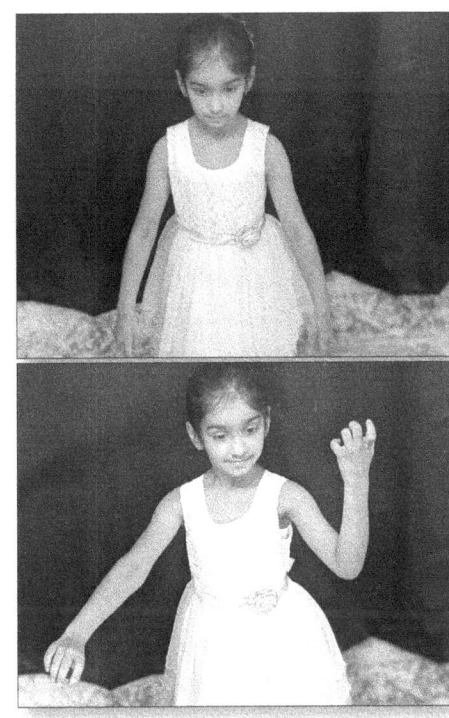
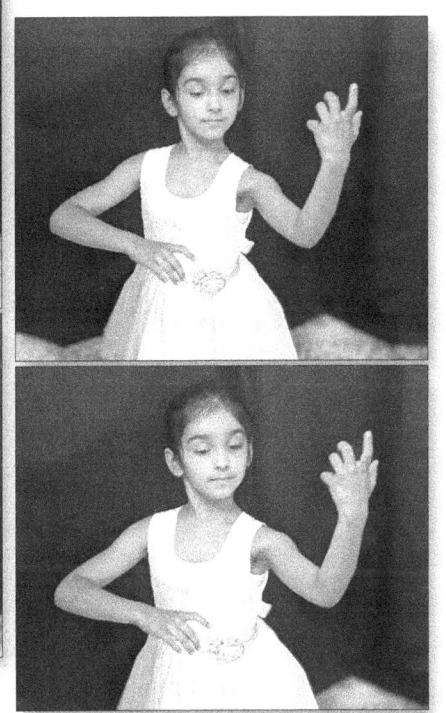

Shoulder Friend

The last step of the Earn Your Violin sequence is placing the box violin (see "Placing the Box Violin" on page 50).

A soft stuffed animal can be used with very young students as a precursor to the box violin. The ideal animal is compact, moderately firm, and slightly taller than the height of the child's neck. This allows the child to experience the physical sensation of their pressing motion.

This friendly activity provides a soft and inviting way to learn to hold an object between the shoulder and jawbone.

EARNING THE BOW

While the child is working to earn their bow, practices should include the following components:

- Playing songs on the piano for speed and mastery;
- Learning songs in "cello position" (see page 32)
- Placing and stabilizing the violin on the shoulder;
- Playing songs "tandem" style (see page 55);
- Bowholds and bow exercises (covered in the next two chapters); and
- Note-reading activities from the *Lines & Spaces* book, once introduced.

Because playing with the violin in shoulder position will be more physically fatiguing than other activities, this part of practice will not take a majority of the practice time ... even though your child will be excited to be finally playing. As your child builds stamina for the violin position, you should plan to spend most of the practice time on the other activities listed above.

As your child reviews already-known songs on the piano and violin, you will notice many kinds of progress:

- Making fewer mistakes;
- Being able to play the full song without errors the first time around, instead of taking a few tries to get it right;
- Being able to play it several times in a row without mistakes;
- Playing it faster and with more accurate rhythm; and
- Being able to play it even when they are not concentrating fully (e.g. while looking around or talking to you).

Reviewing already-learned songs on piano and violin is time well-spent. The better your child knows each song, the more of their attention can be devoted to other aspects of playing — e.g. keeping a straight bow, maintaining good posture, making a beautiful tone, and refining their coordination.

Additional "Earn the Bow" Activities

The Open Strings: Eek, Eek the Ants

The youngest children tend to find the terms "Baby string," "Mommy string," "Daddy string," and "Grandpa string" more relatable and memorable than the alphabetic names.

When the child is ready for the alphabetic names, use the verse below. Pluck the corresponding violin string while saying each word in bold. Be sure the child realizes that "Eek" starts with E, "Ant" starts with "A," and so on; and that these letters match the string name.

> **Eek, Eek, Eek**, all the little
> **Ants, Ants, Ants**, digging in the
> **Dirt, Dirt, Dirt**, going under-
> **Ground, Ground, Ground**.

Violists can use the verse: "Ants, Ants, Ants, digging in the Dirt, Dirt, Dirt, going under-Ground, Ground, Ground, looking for some Cake, Cake, Cake."

String Patterns

The parent speaks a pattern of 3-4 string names; the child plucks each pattern. This reinforces the names of the strings.

Begin with easy patterns such as, "E, E, A." Gradually make the patterns more complicated.

Play the Secret Code

The parent says 3 finger numbers; the student plucks them in cello position on the D string. This builds finger independence and awareness of the numerical finger names.

Begin with easy patterns such as "1, 1, 1." Once these are mastered, move to two-note patterns such as "1, 2, 1" or "1, 4, 1." Next, move to patterns with three different numbers. Last, specify "A string" or "D string" for each pattern.

The child's progress on this game will depend on their working memory, their ability to locate each finger, and their facility with pressing the fingers.

Crack the Code

The parent taps finger-to-thumb in a three-note pattern, or plucks three notes on the violin. The child names notes indicated using solfège.

Begin with patterns of repeated notes (e.g. "*do-do-do*"). Introduce patterns with two notes when the child is ready.

Treasure Hunt

This exercise builds the muscle memory for holding the violin. Use a box violin in the beginning, and do the activity in a carpeted room.

Place the violin into playing position. Then have the child walk a short distance to retrieve a small item or perform a task. Examples include picking up a pen, putting it back, touching a doorknob, opening a drawer, and putting something away.

Check the child's posture and violin position after each task. Make sure the body is tall and the violin has not slid out of place. In the beginning the violin will need to be placed "from scratch" after each task.

CHAPTER 3

PREPARING THE BOWHOLD

,

PLACING THE VIOLIN

For students approximately 6 years old and older, this section will serve as the introduction to the violin position and creating the bowhold.

For younger students, this section builds upon the activities and skills introduced in the previous chapter, including the Movement Building Block sequence.

IN THIS SECTION:

Forming the Bowhold on a Pencil

This method of creating the bowhold tailors the bowhold to the individual student's hand shape.

NOTE: A hexagonal pencil will provide better stability for students than a round one, even though the hexagonal angles are steeper than those of the octagonal bow.

Students who seem a bit unstable on the hexagonal pencil may benefit from using a Ticonderoga Tri-write™ pencil. The triangular design can provide students with more clarity and stability: 1) The thumb can rest on the flat bottom surface; and 2) The pinky has a dedicated, large surface area "behind" the stick, allowing it to feel more stable.

① Hold the pencil upright in the left hand (violin hand), by the eraser end.

② Form a tall "egg" between the middle finger of the right hand and the thumb.

If needed, practice these three shapes with the right hand:

1. Bird's beak (thumb and finger straight);
2. Circle (thumb and finger rounded); and
3. Egg (thumb and fingers pulled toward the palm).

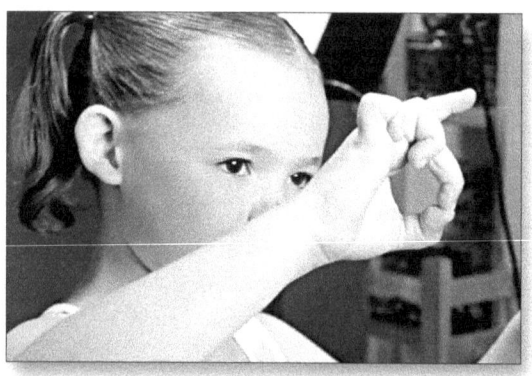

③ Use the violin hand to line up the pencil with the knuckles of the back of the bow hand. *This helps ensure that the angle of the pencil is matched to the angle of the hand.*

④ Keeping the pencil on this same angle, roll it over the top of the hand, open the "egg," and insert between the thumb and middle fingertips. Make sure the wrist is straight, that the thumb and finger still form an egg, and that the pencil is resting on the *tip* of the thumb. *The egg has hatched. Now we see a bird sitting on a branch!*

It works best if the hand is at chest level, and the elbow hanging below, so that the wrist is straight. (The student in the illustration below should drop the elbow a bit lower.)

Keep holding the pencil with the violin hand, so the birds feel safe and secure.

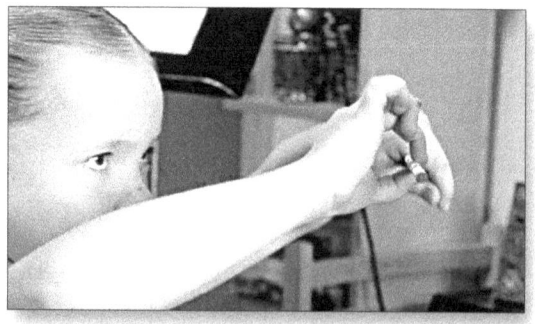

⑤ Drop the ring finger next to the middle finger in a place that feels natural. *The bird's sister or brother comes and sits next to it on the branch!*

While these fingers may be spaced close together for some students, this should not be over-emphasized. Striving to push them together will introduce undesirable tension in the hand, creating imbalances later on.

⑥ Allow the index and pinky fingers to fall onto the pencil in a natural way, also on the fingertips. *Two birdie friends come sit next to the brother and sister.*

There should be a little extra space between fingers 1-2 and 3-4. Have the child blow air through these spaces — they enjoy this.

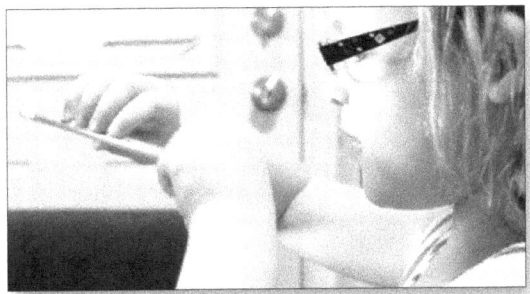

⑦ Drop the middle two fingers over the front of the pencil, keeping them curved while doing so. The index and pinky should remain on their tips. *The amount of draping should be whatever is comfortable for the child's hand.*

- The middle finger *may* slightly touch the fingernail side of the thumb.
- The two middle fingers are now "snuggling" around the front of the pencil.
- We can also say that the "ducks" have only their feet in the water — approximately to the first knuckle joint. Make sure not to push them all the way underwater.

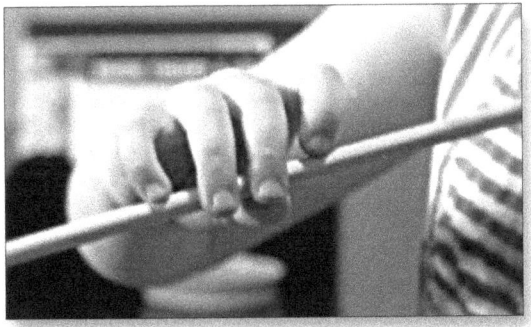

⑧ Lift and extend the index finger off the pencil. *One of the bird friends flies away.* Now drop it down onto the pencil, with the tip curved slightly around the front. *Look! There is "Mama bear" asleep by the pond. Her paw drapes over the log. The thumb is baby bear, safe in the cave.* Observe these details:

- The pencil should rest in the first fold of the finger, not on the second fold. *Make sure mama bear doesn't fall into the water!*
- The index will be slightly on the side (leaning), rather than on the bottom (perpendicular). *Mama Bear is a side sleeper, not a tummy sleeper.*
- There should be a slight space between the middle finger and the index. *This is the window that lets light into the cave.*

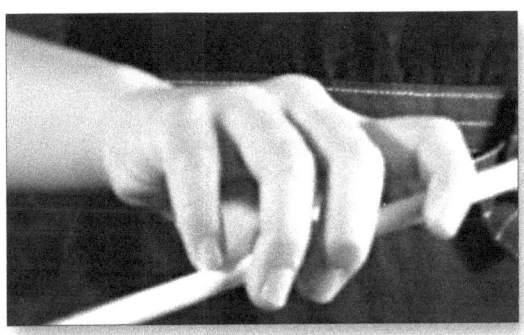

⑨ Rotate the hand so that you are looking at the index side of the bowhold. Do the thumb and index finger form a "C" shape? *This is the bear cave.*

Also check to make sure that the pinky has TWO good corners, and the thumb has ONE good corner. ("Do you have three good corners? Let's count.") *Little bear (the thumb) needs to stay in his cave, standing up. If he walks out to the pond, the ducks might run away.*

Bow Finger Pressure

The student will need to learn to calibrate the amount of firmness of their bowhold. Too little and the fingers will slip-slide around. Too much and their bowhold will be rigid and stressed-out.

One a scale of 1–10, if 1 is "cooked spaghetti noodle" and 10 is "death grip," the ideal pressure is about 5. On average, young children tend toward being overly loose.

Flapping the Wings

This important exercise builds flexibility and control in the bowhold, so that it is both supple and stable while playing. Once introduced it should be practiced daily throughout Book 1, since the bowhold will continue evolving throughout the first year of playing.

Once your child has established a quick, reliable bowhold on the pencil, this exercise will ensure that they have the agility and awareness to maintain this once they are actually playing with the bow.

The skill is keeping the index curved while the pinky extends. Doing this is challenging because our fingers like to copy each other!

Perform the following steps using a hexagonal pencil:

1. Begin with a perfect bowhold. Make sure the pinky is on the back face of the pencil. *The helper hand can hold the end of the pencil in the beginning if desired for stability, but should be retired when the student is ready.*

2. Make sure the wrist is *straight*. The elbow will be slightly below the hand.

3. Extend the pinky (release its curve). The pinky fingertip should keep its spot on the pencil, and not "hop" or lift. A gentle extension is best (not all the way straight). *The little bird is spreading its wings.*

4. As the pinky extends, the thumb must extend as well. *Little bear is waking up and stretching.*

5. Make sure the index (pointer) finger does *not* extend. *Mama bear stays sleeping with her paw over the log.* The index should always contact the pencil on

the first fold. *Mama bear has her paw, not her elbow, around the log.*

6. Finally, re-curve the pinky finger and the thumb.

The arm and wrist should remain still. The bowhold should be soft enough to be supple, but firm enough that the fingers do not slip around. In other words, the student should observe a constant, slight pressure on their thumb.

When ready, perform a set of four extension-retractions, then check the bowhold ("One, two, three, CHECK"). Now say, "Count your corners." The student should look:

1. Does my pinky have TWO corners?

2. Does my thumb have ONE corner?

3. Is my index finger still folded on the first ("paw") line?

Re-set the bowhold as needed and repeat. The pace of the movement should always be slow and controlled, which builds a more conscious mind-to-body connection and a higher quality of movement.

This exercise should be practiced many times a day for several weeks to build muscle memory, so it becomes natural and effortless. When the child is ready, they should do this exercise *without* the helper hand — always on a pencil.

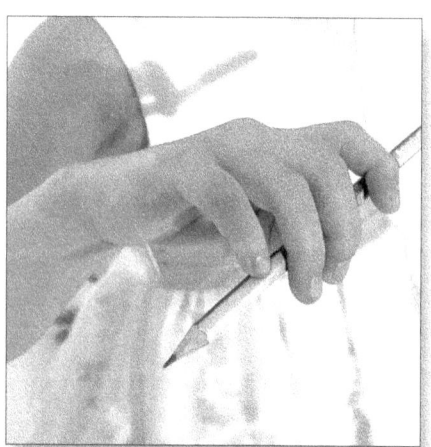
Begin with a perfect bowhold, with the pinky behind the pencil.

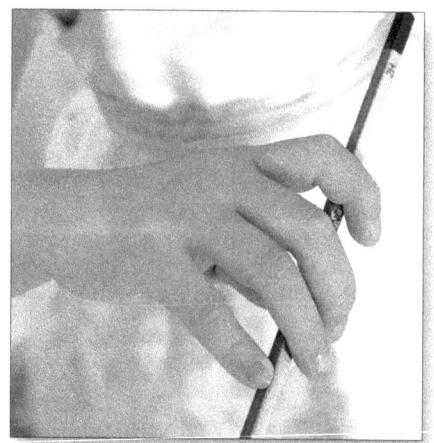
Release or extend the pinky. It should touch the pencil the whole time. The index (pointer) should stay curved.

Re-curve the pinky and thumb to return to the original bowhold.

Bow Slide

Bow slides help the child experience straight bowing and develop flexibility and responsiveness in their bowhold. Take a quick look at the photos below to get the basic idea of the bow slide. The positions of the bow arm when practicing with this tool are:

- *The starting square.* The elbow forms a right angle, and the wrist is FLAT. The hand is approximately level with the chest. The elbow hangs slightly *below* the wrist.

- *Extend.* The hand slides away from the body. We'll call this an *out-bow*. The wrist will bend as the hand is pulled down. The bow pinky should extend *passively*. This motion was prepared in "Flapping the Wings," page 46.

- *Square.* The hand is returned to its starting position. The wrist lifts up, flattening the forearm shape. The pinky and thumb should re-curve. *Re-curving these fingers is a conscious, active motion.*

- *Shoulder.* The child moves their hand toward their shoulder. We'll call this an *in-bow*. Their bowhold will stay the same; the wrist will take a convex shape.

Young children may naturally twist in the direction of the bow arm. Help them to keep their shoulders aligned with their feet and their "lighthouse" (sternum) pointed forward, between their toes. *See page 49 for more posture details.*

Slide on the bow to the rhythm of the solfège words — i.e. the *notes* of the song, rather than the lyrics. The hand should change direction on each syllable.

① Use a dowel rod that is several inches longer than the child's bow and approximately the same thickness. Wrap a piece of paper around the dowel and tape the seam. A length of a bubble tea drinking straw, approximately 5 inches (12 cm), could also be used.

The child will form a bowhold on the paper and use this to slide up and down the "bow."

② The child makes a "little v" with their left hand to receive the top of the dowel (not pictured). This is preparation for supporting the violin. The parent holds the bow at approximately a 45° angle to the child's body, with a downward slope.

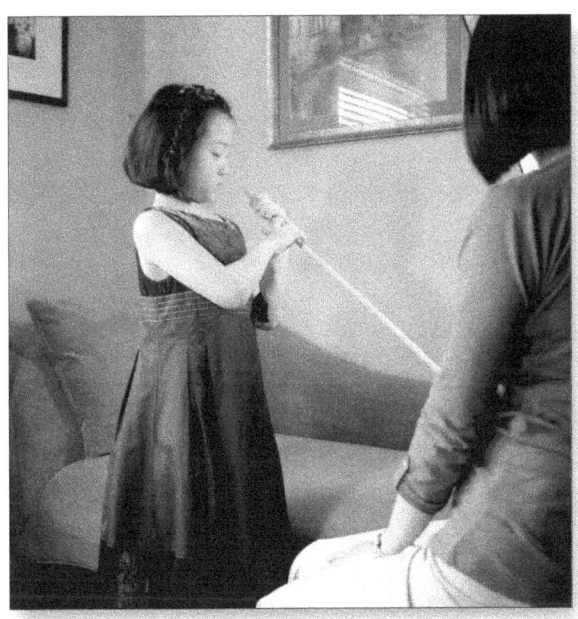

③ The wrist will naturally bend downward as the hand approaches the floor. As the child's hand returns to starting position, the wrist needs to lift upward in order to return to a "flat" position.

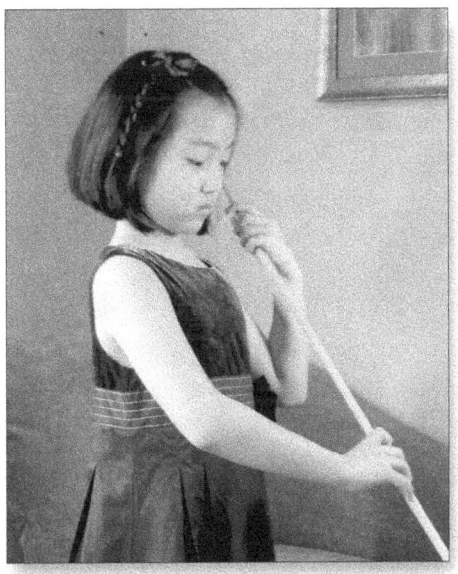

④ Correct the bowhold and wrist position before beginning each song, and perhaps occasionally during the song if the child is amenable to correction.

Making a Bowhold on the Bow

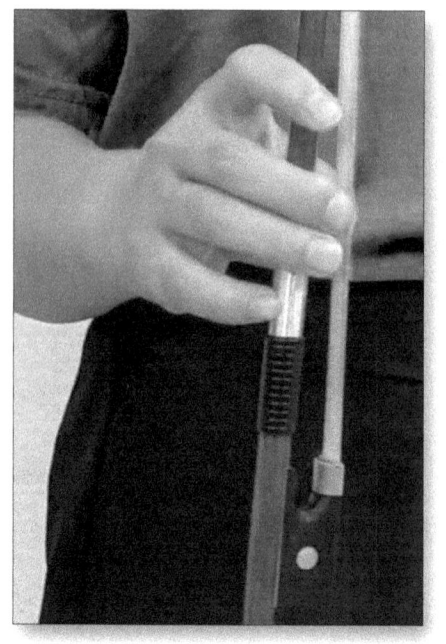

The initial bowhold is formed at the edge between the silver wrap and the stick.

Your teacher will introduce bowholds on the bow when your child can quickly and accurately form the bowhold on a pencil.

Practice on carpet so the child does not worry about dropping the bow. Observe the following details:

- Beginners should place their "egg" where the silver wrap meets the wooden bow stick. This saves the pinky from supporting the full weight of the bow at this early stage.

- The thumb will lightly touch the bow hair just below the fingernail.

- If the thumb doesn't touch the hair, it might need to bend more. Alternatively, the hand might be rotated too far over the front of the bow. Ask the student to keep their hand *behind* instead of *on top of* the bow.

- *Continue holding the bow near the silver wrap for the first few months to maintain the bowhold in perfect form.* As the bowhold becomes more secure, it may be relocated down to its final position next to the frog.

- The fingers should rest lightly on the stick.

Maintaining the Bowhold

Maintaining a good bowhold requires significantly greater automaticity (i.e. muscle memory) than simply making one in the first place. The many bow exercises in this book are designed to strengthen the student's tactile awareness, finger independence and control, finger strength, and muscle memory. These exercises are equally valuable for older and younger students.

Practice the bowhold challenges starting on page 58 for several weeks before playing any scales or songs with the bow.

Progressive Bow Hand Placements

When practicing any of the load-bearing exercises with the bowhold, use the following hand placements to maintain correct form while gradually increasing pinky strength. Advance to the next step when the current stage is easy and accurate:

1. Bow thumb on the top edge of the silver wrap (slightly below the balance point);

2. Bowhold between the silver wrap and black thumb leather;

3. Final position (at the frog).

Beware: The Kitty Litter Box

Never place the thumb inside the curved cut-out opening in the frog.

We will call this the "kitty litter box," ew!

This space is too narrow and doesn't allow the thumb to bend.

PREPARING THE VIOLIN POSITION

Foot Position

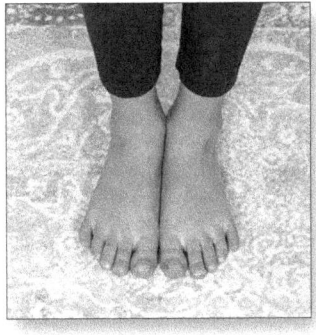 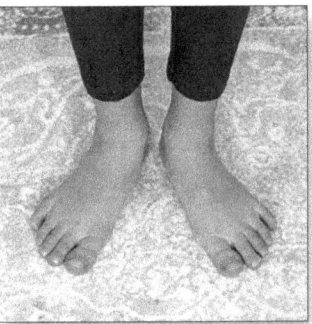 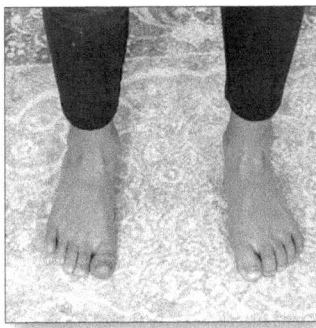 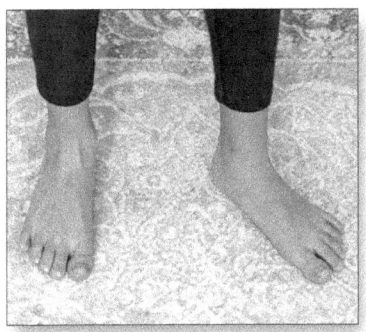

Place the feet together.	Open the toes into a "V."	Open the heels. Now the feet are even again.	Turn or step the violin foot *slightly* to the left.

Spine, Torso and Head Alignment

The following exercises establish awareness of the alignment of the body. This core alignment will be essential for correctly placing the violin.

Find your breath

Inhale and exhale deeply to "sense into" the inner space of the torso. The breath is the easiest way to feel this space. Notice the expansion in both the front and back of the body. The torso must remain aligned and open when the violin is placed.

Purpose: This awareness activity helps prevent students from collapsing forward when the violin is placed.

Find your treetop

Sense into the "treetop" (top of the head). The teacher or parent may touch the top of the head to assist. Connecting proprioceptively with this point allows the student to keep this aligned with the tailbone. Feel the spine lengthen as the treetop reaches toward the sky.

Purpose: This helps prevent the tendency for the head to reach toward the left or fall toward the chest in an effort to hold the violin.

"Watching Owl"

Practice turning just the head while keeping the body still.

Purpose: This helps prevent the tendency for students to rotate their body when turning their head, causing them to twist left while playing.

Feet, Shoulders, and Lighthouse

Find the center of the sternum. This is the student's "Lighthouse." Imagine the light shining directly forward toward the teacher or parent (exactly between the feet).

Purpose: This helps prevent the tendency to twist to the left when students place the violin or cross the midline with the bow arm. Finding their Lighthouse allows students to consciously re-align their body.

Placing the Box Violin

Prepare the feet and body, using the steps on page 49.

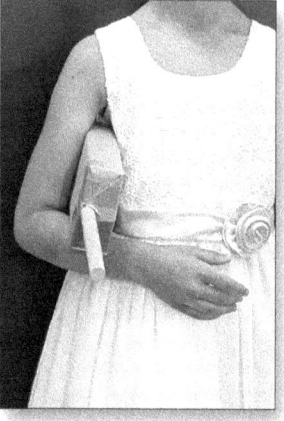

Place the box violin in "rest position."

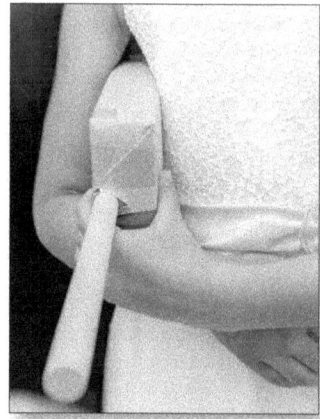

Grasp the lower shoulder of the box with the left hand.

Bring the box violin in front of the body.

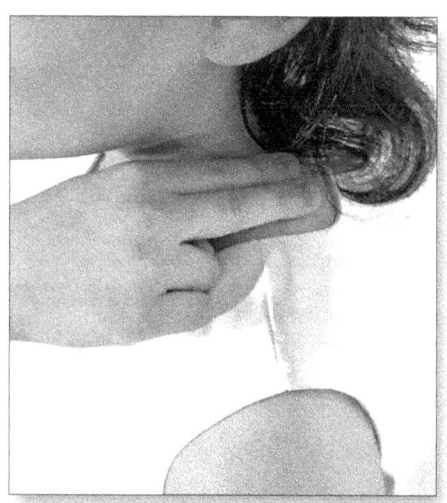

Pat the "Shoulder Nest," the corner where the trapezius meets the neck.

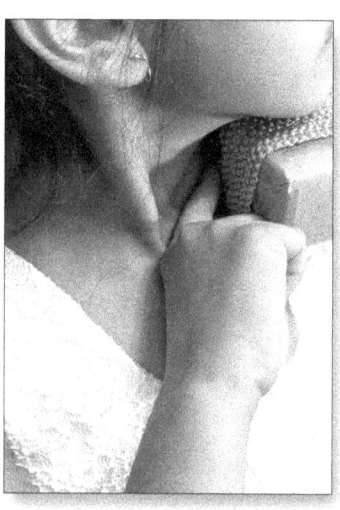

Place the violin onto this spot, and "snuggle" it into the neck.

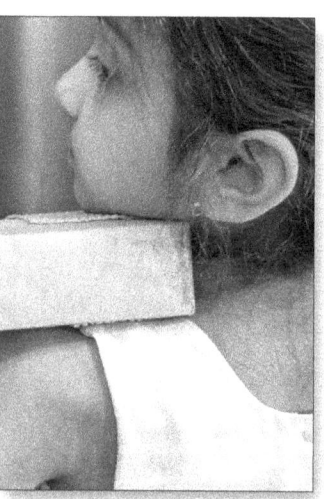

Turn the head slightly and rest the jawbone on the box.

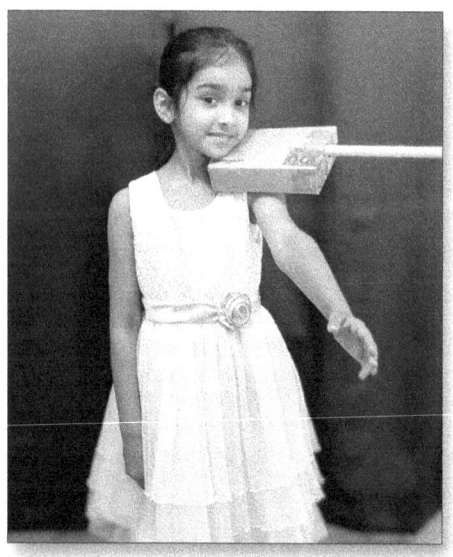

Swingset

Relax the violin arm to the side of the body. Swing this arm while holding the violin with the head. *The parent or teacher should position their hand nearby under neck of the (box) violin, as a safety net to help the child feel more at ease.*

Initially the violin will quickly become wobbly when the child swings their arm. Over time they will become more accurate in placing the violin, and more skillful in gently anchoring the violin with their head. To achieve this, practice placing the violin many times during each violin practice.

The "Treasure Hunt" activity may now be introduced (see page 41).

Placing the Violin

Prepare the feet and body (see page 49). Place the violin in rest position.

Grasp the lower shoulder of the violin with the left hand.

Bring the violin in front of the body.

Rotate the violin upward.

Place the violin into the shoulder corner and snuggle it into the neck.

Swingset: Swing the left arm while supporting the violin.

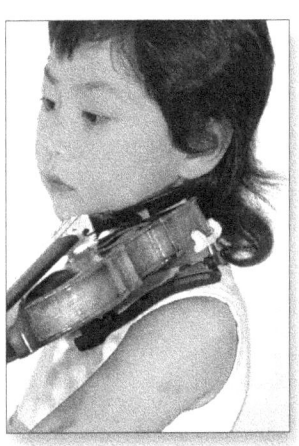

The jaw rests on the chinrest, with the head approximately vertical.

Balloon Ride

Discovering the "violin 'v'" as a source of support for the action of the left hand

Use the "violin 'v'" to slightly raise and lower the violin. Do this each time the student places the violin for a few weeks.

POSTURE & BOWHOLD

Adjusting the Shoulder Rest and Chinrest

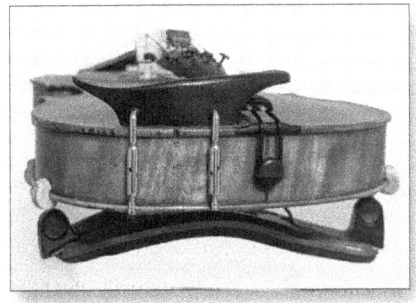

If using a sponge or shoulder rest, the less elevated side will go opposite the chinrest: "Thin side, chin side."

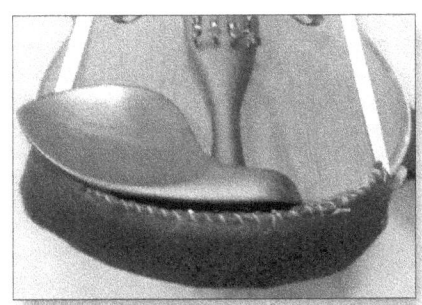

A chinrest cover may be used to cover any area that causes discomfort. Moleskin, a soft fabric with an adhesive backing, is found in grocery stores and can be used to cover the metal brackets.

Moleskin received its name from its original material — the soft leather of ground-moles.

Two Methods for Placing the Fingering Hand

Option 1: The Lowercase "v"

The violin is placed in the triangular "v" shape easel formed by the left hand ("v" for "violin"). The thumb is activated only just enough to maintain the "v." The thumb tip is relaxed and does not grip the neck.

After placing the violin, the "v" can slightly release (and open). The violin will rest on the end of the lower thumb bone and the base knuckle of the pointer finger. Have the student palpate these two knobs to tangibly experience these points of support.

Make a lower case "v" by closing the thumb to the hand.

Place this "v" behind the first finger tape. The violin rests in the "v" the way a ball rests in the crook of two tree branches.

The thumb can now soften, resting lightly on the violin neck. Fold the fingertip to the E string. *At this stage it is okay if the wrist touches the violin.*

Option 2: The Finger Square

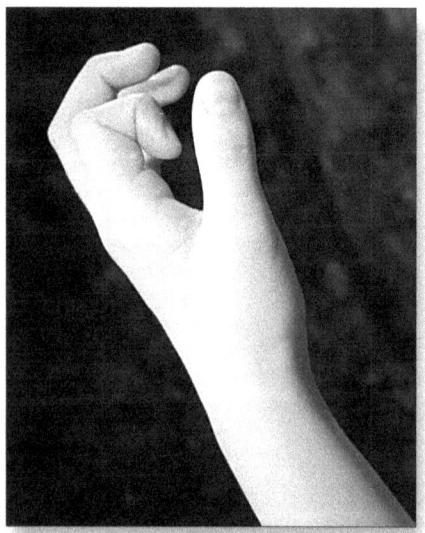

Make a compact square with the index. Wiggle the other fingers (including the thumb) to loosen and release them.

Place the tip of the first finger square on the fingerboard, on the E string.

The top of the knuckle should be parallel with the fingerboard. This means the hand is neither too high nor too low.

Make sure the base knuckle of the first finger is "tucked"; the finger should be aligned with the hand. Stroke the back of the finger; you should barely feel the knuckle.

Notes of the Scale

At this stage of learning we want each finger to play only *one* note.

The fingers are numbered 1 (index), 2, 3, and 4 (pinky). The thumb is not included, since it does not play any notes.

There are a total of 8 notes in the scale. So the fingers will be assigned according to the chart on the right:

Finger	D string	A string
1	*do*	*so*
2	*re*	*la*
3	*mi*	*ti*
4	*fa*	high *do*

Rotating to the D String

for older beginners and adult students

It is fine in the beginning for the student to simply open the first finger square slightly to reach to the D string. In this case the elbow will point straight down. This is technically an A string arm angle.

Some older beginners may be able to rotate the arm inward toward the midline to the correct D string position. The hand rotates with the elbow, "carrying" the fingers to the D string.

There are two visual cues for the D string elbow from the student's point of view:

* The student will be able to see the edge of their left forearm through the "window" of the violin C-bout.
* The bottom fold of the first finger will hover over or touch the E string (see picture below).

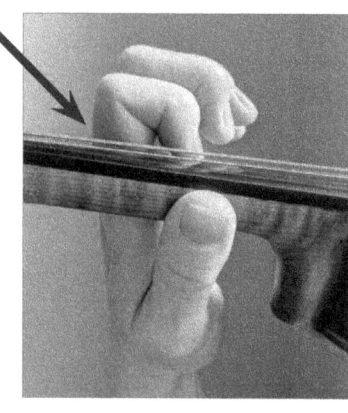 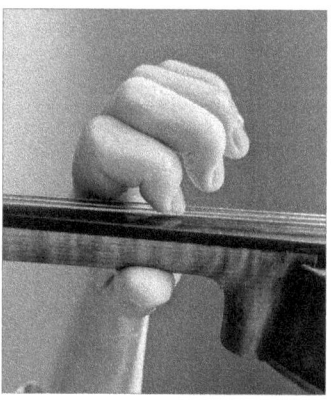  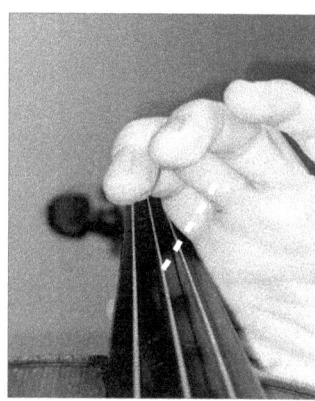

E string: The bottom fold of the first finger is aligned with the top of the fingerboard.

D string: The bottom fold rotates over the fingerboard, ending overtop the E string.

E string (front view): The bottom fold is aligned with the top of the fingerboard.

D string (front view): The bottom fold is rotated over the E string.

Tandem Violin

If your child is age 4-7, the child will move the fingers while the parent plucks or draws the bow. If they are age 8 or older, your teacher may permit them to bow independently after the first few tries.

Most children have a strong desire for independence and will express a strong preference that the parent refrain from adjusting their posture or guiding their bow. However, many violin skills require gentle adjustments to ensure that they are learned correctly.

Let your child know they can "earn" their independence by showing you what a great job they do remembering the desired skills and posture during this initial stage.

DO-DO-RE-RE-DO

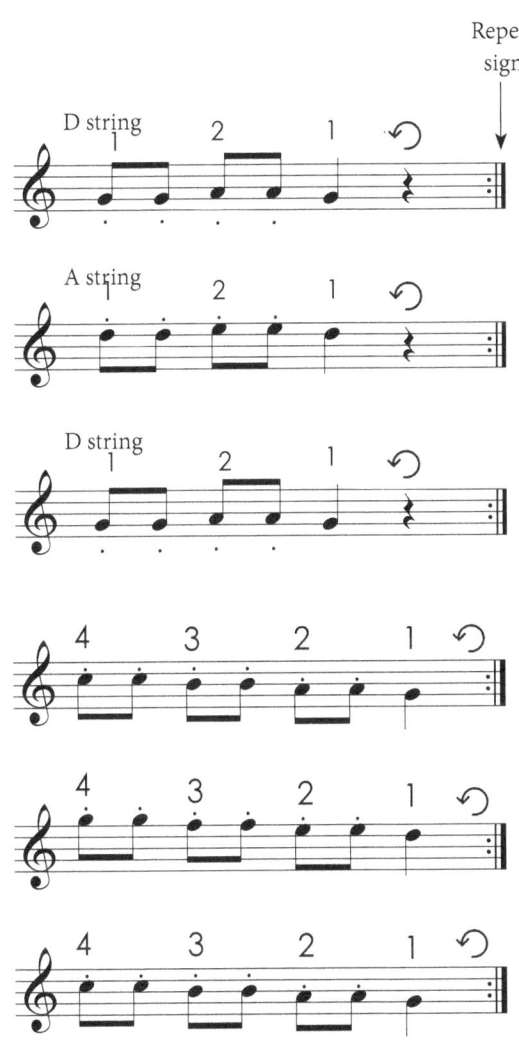

Do the pattern at right on the middle two strings. *When playing second finger, the first finger should rest on the string.*

Gravity is always pulling the violin down, so during this early phase the child should compensate by lifting the violin upward (using the "violin v") on each new note.

There should be a distinct pause between each note, with the bow coming to a complete stop. The ↺ sign indicates a counterclockwise bow circle (if using the bow).

NOTE: It is best not the let the child do their own plucking, since this encourages incorrect posture (they will pivot the violin forward).

4433221

The teacher may introduce this exercise first, at their discretion.

1. Place the first finger. Check the angle of the elbow and make sure the fingertip is landing on the thumb-side corner.
2. Place the remaining fingers, in order: 2, 3, 4.
3. Remove the fingers one at a time to play the exercise, hovering the fingers over the string once they lift ("umbrella fingers").

Play this pattern on the middle two strings. The parent again plucks or draws the bow. As always during this initial learning phase, lift the violin slightly on each note to counteract the effect of gravity.

Posture Reminders

- Stand with "violin feet" (see page 49).
- The body is tall and energized.
- The violin rests on the shoulder, not the chest.
- The midline of the violin fingerboard is level with the floor.
- Front edge of the violin is slightly lower than the back.

- The head turns *slightly* to the left.
- The head is nearly vertical, with a *slight* tilt toward the left ear.
- The first finger forms a fairly compact square. The base joint is nearly flat where it meets the back of the hand.
- The wrist and hand form a straight line.

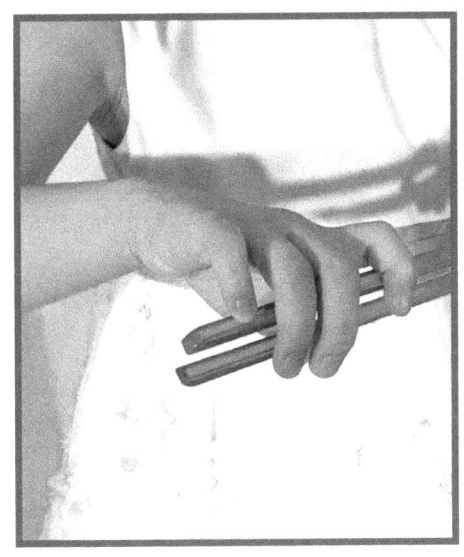

CHAPTER 4

KINESTHETIC EXERCISES

TO DEVELOP THE BOW HAND & BOW ARM

IN THIS SECTION:

Bow Hand Awareness, Strength, & Agility

Pinky & Index Taps
Thumb Presses
Duck Splashes

These movement exercises build tactile and muscle memory for the finger placements and "touch points" of the index, pinky, middle fingers, and thumb.

Support the pencil with the violin hand. Tap or pulse the fingers in the order below. Perform a set of four movements, then check the bowhold to make sure it is still perfect. *Keep the hand aligned with the arm as much as possible.*

1. **Pinky:** The correct pinky placement is on the *top inner* surface of the hexagonal pencil. Tap strong enough that the "helper hand" feels the vibration.

2. **Index:** Tap the mama bear on her "snuggle spot." She should sleep on her side, not her tummy.

3. **Thumb:** Continue using the helper hand to stabilize the pencil. Squeeze and release the thumb four times. The index and middle fingers will receive and oppose the thumb pressure. Keep the pinky relaxed.

4. **Middle Fingers ("Duck Splashes"):** Hop the middle fingers on and off the pencil, keeping them curved. Make sure the index stays folded over the pencil.

For each movement above, check the following dimensions for both the active and the resting fingers: 1) The shape of the finger; 2) the finger's location on the stick (i.e. spacing); and 3) the stick's location on the finger (i.e. contact point).

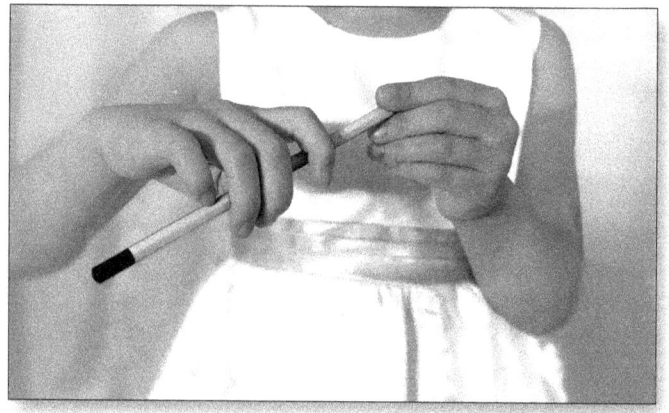

Begin with a correct bowhold. Use the helper hand to support the pencil. Keep the hand aligned with the arm.

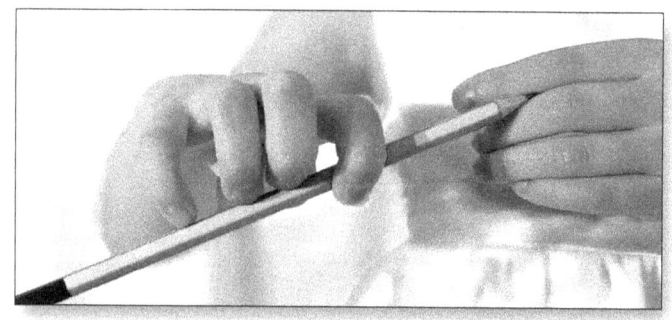

Duck Splashes: Hop the middle fingers on and off the pencil, keeping them curved. Make sure the index stays folded over the pencil.

Hand Rotation

A "falling over" pinky can be caused by lack of pinky control, or by a hand that is leaning the wrong direction, or both. These exercises help students understand the angular dimension of bowhold.

Doorknob

Consciously control the pronation or supination of the hand.

Practice changing the angle of the bow hand from flat (Mama Bear on her tummy) to pronated (Mama Bear sleeping on her side) and back. The final (correct) angle should be approximately 45° of pronation. The elbow must be slightly lifted to achieve this counterclockwise tilt.

Wobbly Bird

Awareness and control of the angle of the pinky.

Practice tilting the bow pinky to the side, then standing it back up again.

The correct angle for playing purposes is perpendicular to the bow stick.

Flapping the Wings (see page 46)

Dynamic stability in the bow hand and ability of the pinky to re-curve after playing at the tip.

Extend the pinky ("little bird"), keeping the first finger ("mama bear") snuggled around the stick. The thumb and the fingers adjacent to the pinky will extend somewhat, as well. *The helper hand may be used initially for stability if helpful.*

The "touch points" of each finger should remain the same throughout— there should be minimal rolling on the pencil. Be sure to use an hexagonal (not round) pencil.

Do three sets of four, pausing between sets to check the pinky curve, touch points, and shape inside the hand. This exercise is practiced throughout the first year of study.

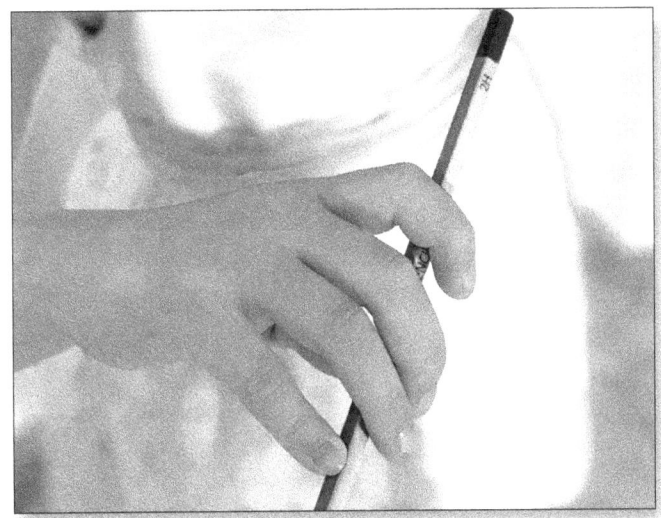

Chopstick pinky

This exercise builds strength in and awareness of the pinky.

Select a training chopstick with square legs. Make the bowhold on the chopstick with the pinky toward the open side. Use the pinky to close the chopsticks with a tapping sound.

The target skills are 1) maintaining the pinky in a curved shape, and 2) making sure it stays perpendicular and upright, rather than falling sideways. Some muscular engagement is needed for this.

Complete three sets of 10 pinky presses each day. As the pinky gains strength (over several months' time), move gradually higher on the chopstick. The exercise is complete when the pinky presses are easy and accurate with the hand at the "closed" end of the chopstick.

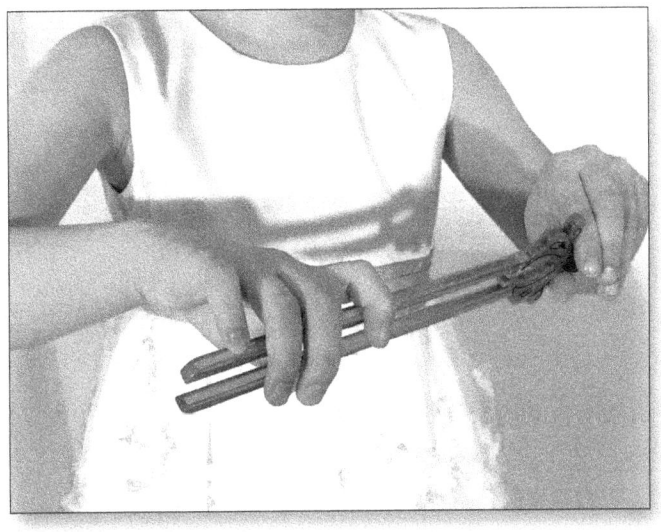

Bow Hand Awareness, Strength, & Agility

Up Like a Rocket

Maintaining the bowhold in the presence of distraction.

Create a perfect bowhold and begin with the bow vertical. Say the rhyme below, with the accompanying motions. Place a shallow milk cap on the tip for an extra challenge.

Up like a rocket, down like the rain,	*Raise the bow high quickly, then lower it slowly.*
Back and forth like a choo-choo train,	*Move the bow side-to-side (make sure the body stays still).*
Round and round like a great big sun,	*Tip of the bow traces a large circle (the bow is still vertical).*
Round and round like a great big drum,	*Trace a horizontal circle, like stirring soup.*
Up on your head like a unicorn,	*Touch the frog of the bow to the forehead.*
Two-bump pinky, and a one-bump thumb.	*Bring the bowhold toward the face to check pinky and thumb.*

Animal Climb

Strengthening the bow pinky; connecting the index and thumb.
Supplies: An animal finger puppet, or a similar small, soft object.

The student holds the bow vertically while the teacher or parent uses a finger puppet to climb the bow stick from middle to the tip, applying gentle pressure. The higher the animal gets, the harder the opposing fingers must work.

The animal doesn't want to fall out of the tree, so it jumps off as soon as the bow leans or becomes wobbly.

Hair Side: Pressure on this side helps the child pair the index (pointer) and the thumb — the "bear hug" action of the hand. While these fingers are strong and the animal will easily reach the top, repetition helps to build muscle memory.

Stick Side: Pressure on this side builds pinky strength. This is much more strenuous! The animal will be excited to receive an (imaginary) treat when it reaches the top, which may take 4–8 weeks.

Silent Bear Hug

Training the connection between the index and thumb, for sound production.

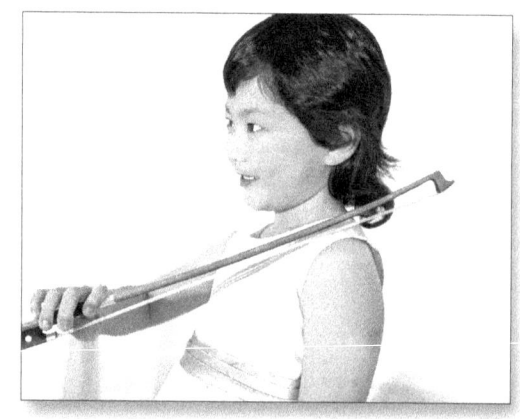

1. Make a perfect bowhold.
2. Rest the bow on the opposite shoulder (or on the violin), with the bow arm in a square.
3. Press and release the index, using the thumb to resist. This will close the gap between the bow stick and the hair. The other fingers should stay relaxed, and the elbow should hang as relaxed as possible. *The index is mama bear, and the thumb is baby bear. They are hugging through the stick.*
4. Later, with the violin, do four silent bear hugs on each string, starting with just D & A. Notice which muscles you feel working at each different angle.

Clock Hands

Building pinky strength.

Create a perfect bowhold at the student's current bow placement.

Rotate the bow from 11:00 (almost perpendicular to the floor) to 9:00 (parallel to the floor) using the forearm. Do three sets of four.

Bouncing Branch

Building pinky strength.

Create a bowhold at the student's current bow placement. Hold the bow horizontally (parallel to the floor). Bounce the bow rapidly four times up and down. *A raccoon is trying to shake the birds off the branch!* Do three sets of four.

Preparation for Rebounds

Tree Trunk

Aligning and balancing the body, balancing the head; and lengthening the spine.

Give the following steps to the student:

1. "Bend your knees slightly, making sure you can still see your toes. The feet should be hip-width apart, and the arms slightly lifted from the sides."

2. "Imagine your tailbone sinking down." *This slightly straightens the lower back and aligns the upper body for maximum relaxation.*

3. "Feel the top of your head lifting the body into the sky like a balloon, pulling your upper body tall."

4. "Imagine all the water in your body gently flowing downward. Let your head relax; shoulders; arms; back; pelvis; legs. Feel your body become heavier on your feet. Tell me when you can feel your body get heavier."

Pause and let the child do this work.

5. "I am going to test and see if you are grounded. When I lean on you, take my push and connect it down into the ground."

The parent gently pushes on the right upper arm, toward the midline. If the child's body moves, have them relax and sink their weight down again.

The parent now pushes gently and gradually on the sternum, then between the shoulder blades, and finally the other arm.

Rebounds

Awareness of the dynamic properties of the bow in motion, and stability of the fingers under dynamic load.

First, use "Tree Trunk" (above) to ground the body.

Now hold the bow vertical on the right side of the body, with the arm slightly separated. Pulse (bounce) the arm rapidly to the midline, allowing the arm to "rebound" to its starting position. The entire motion should be completed in a single count. The student's body should stay almost perfectly still. This indicates that the arm is relaxed, and the body is grounded.

Relax the hand after each rebound, and check the bowhold after each set of four. Make sure the index finger doesn't wrap too far around the stick.

NOTE: This exercise places dynamic load on the pinky. For this reason, you should follow the bowhold placements described on the next page.

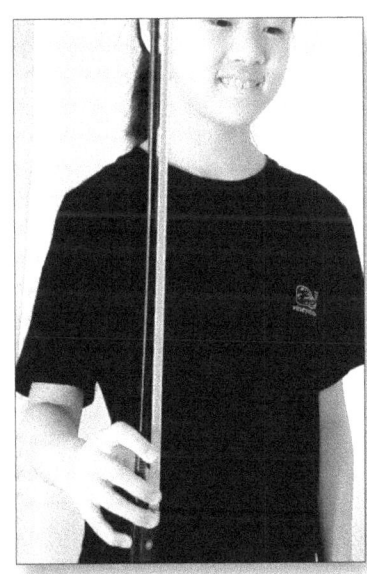 

Bow Spider

This exercise builds strength and independence in the fingers of the bow hand, as well as resilience in the bowhold. It requires a great deal of finger individuation, and should be introduced only when the bowhold is well-trained. It is a fun activity for group class.

Create a bowhold at the frog. Climb up the bow to the middle, then return back. Maintain the correct bowhold contact points for each finger throughout the climb.

ANGLES & MOVEMENT

Skyscraper

Wrist angle for frog, middle, and tip playing.

1. **Ground floor.** Hold the bow vertically on right side of body, near the waist. The arm should be bent in a right angle.

2. **Basement.** Lower the bow (⊓) until the arm is nearly straight. The pinky will release its curve.

3. **Ground floor.** Return (∨) to the starting position. Be sure to re-curve the pinky, and make sure the contact point of the index finger remains the same. *Practice many reps of just steps 2–3, which is the most difficult maneuver!*

4. **Rooftop.** When ready for the next step (possibly the following week), again begin at ground floor. This time raise the arm over the head ("rooftop")(∨) and back to ground floor (⊓).

Practice the motions in a segmented fashion until they are mastered. When ready, integrate them into a continuous motion.

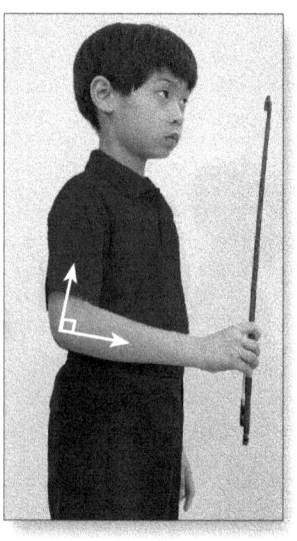 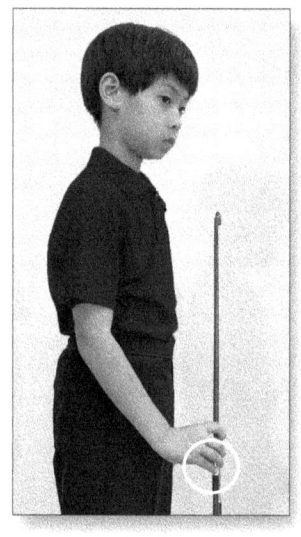 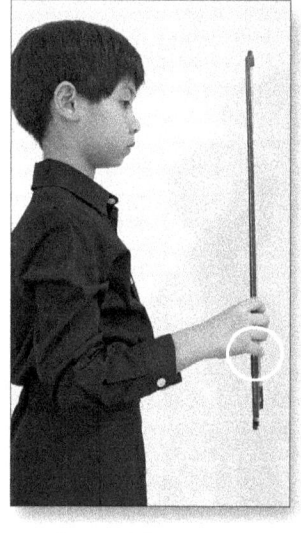 

| Ground floor | Basement | Ground floor | Rooftop |

Stir the Pot

Maintaining the bow vertical, and an "easy" bowhold challenge

Hold the bow vertical. "Stir the pot" using grapefruit-sized circles. Try balancing a shallow bottle cap on the tip of the bow.

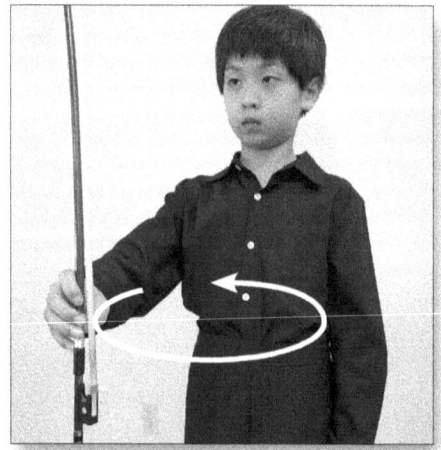

Circle the Moon

Maintaining the bow vertical, awareness of parallel motion, and the "hanging" relationship between hand and elbow.

1. Hold the bow vertically on right side of body, with the hand at face level.

2. Trace large, counter-clockwise circles, making sure the bow doesn't tip forward. *The tip of the bow is circling the moon. Your bow is a candle. Keep it tall and straight ... don't spill the wax!*

3. Make sure the elbow drapes below the arm, and that the pinky stays bent.

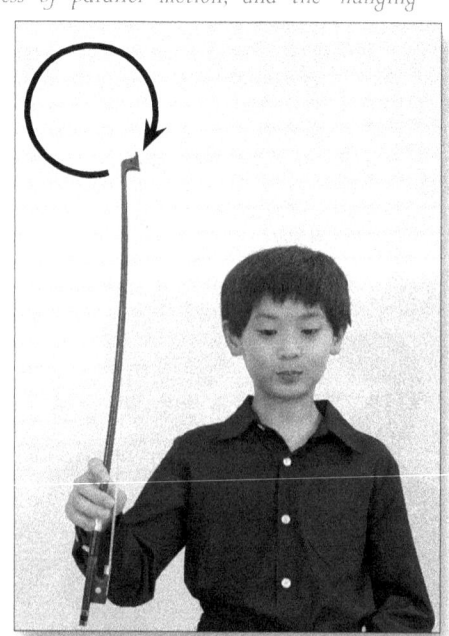

Raise the Drawbridge

Pinky strength and angle, awareness of parallel motion, and the "hanging" relationship between hand and elbow.

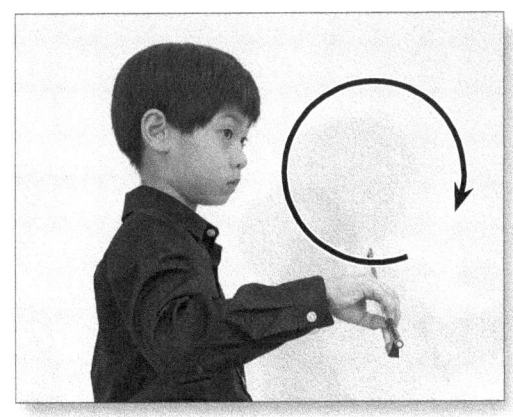

1. Hold the bow horizontally on right side of body, at shoulder level.
2. "Row" the arm forward and down, turning the winch to raise the drawbridge.
3. Make sure the elbow remains below the hand at all times.

Erase the Blackboard

This exercise helps the student understand the concept of moving within a vertical plane.

Near the Wall. The student holds BOTH ends of the bow: one hand holding the screw, the other holding the tip.

Practice moving the bow while staying exactly parallel to the wall: 1) Up and down; 2) Side to side; and 3) In a circular motion.

Above a meterstick. The student stands in their regular practice spot. Place a meterstick on the ground to indicate the plane of the imaginary blackboard. Perform the motions as above, keeping the bow "on" the blackboard (i.e. over the meterstick).

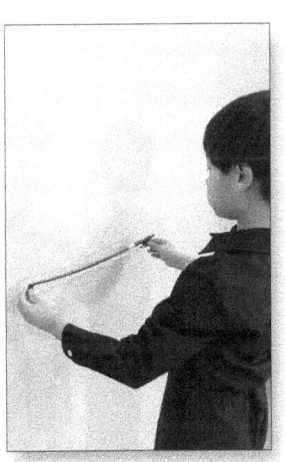  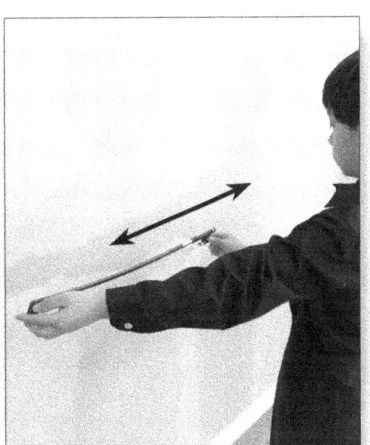 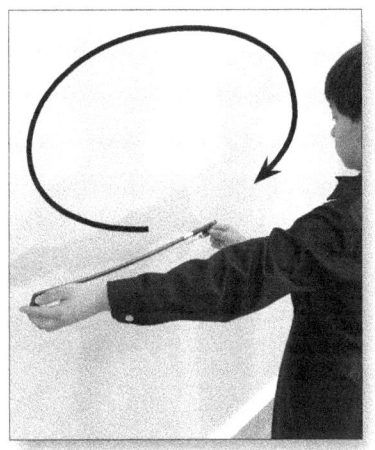

Bow Lasso

Pinky strength, bow angle, proprioception of the bow path, and comfort when playing at the frog.
Prerequisite: Erase the Blackboard (above).

Uniform Speed

1. Turn the head to look at the left shoulder.
2. Rest the bow on the shoulder. It should be slightly angled toward the midline of the body.
3. Circle the bow outward in a counter-clockwise direction, maintaining a consistent speed. This is called a "circle bow" or "retake." The bow should maintain its original angle in both the vertical and side-to-side planes. The student will be continuously managing the path of the bow.

Initially the parent or teacher may need to physically guide the bow by holding the bow on both ends and guiding a few circles to establish the trajectory. The student will "ride" the bow. Gradually yield control to the child.

If needed, hold a large folder or clipboard next to the bow path (near the child's left shoulder) to establish the vertical plane.

continued on the next page

Bow Lasso (cont'd)

Impulse & Inertia

1. Begin with the same starting position as above.

2. Bounce the bow twice on the shoulder. The bounces should be large enough and strong enough to establish proprioception of the full length of the bow.

   Tell the student, "Feel the tip, feel the frog." They can feel the frog directly through touch, and they can sense the springiness of the tip through pressure changes on their index and thumb.

3. On the descent, lasso the bow outward (as before), this time preserving the momentum of the arm.

ANGLES & MOVEMENT

With the Violin & Bow

Deep Sea Dive

Awareness of how the arm creates string crossings; linking hand and elbow.

Raise and lower the arm following the directions below. The arm and hand should move as one unit (like a toy action figure), keeping the pinky curved. The entire motion should be smooth and continuous. A relaxed bow hand will help the string crossing to be silent.

Once the student is playing songs, each string crossing will use a small segment of the "Deep Sea Dive" arc. Make sure there are no "flying fish" (lifting the bow from the string)!

Place the bow on E string, at the square of the arm.	Raise the whole arm (rotate from the ball and socket joint of the shoulder) to silently pivot the bow to G string.	Return to E string, allowing the arm to relax downward with gravity.

Rowing

This exercise builds the awareness needed to adjust the bow lane.

The child pushes the bow laterally back and forth on the string, from the bridge to the edge of the violin body and back. The pinky should stay curved.

 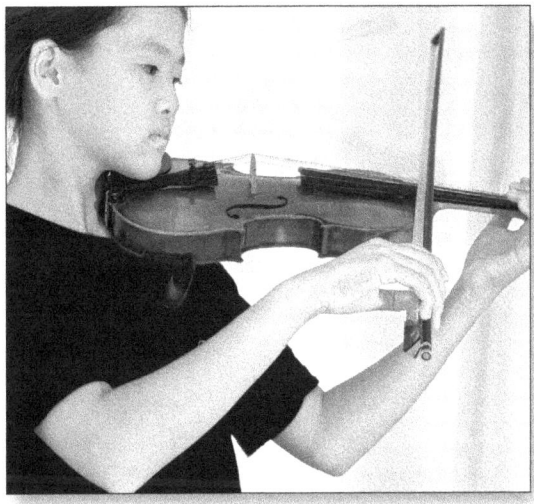

Criss-Cross

Controlling and adjusting the bow angle using the arm. NOTE: This exercise is for the arm, not the bow hand; the pinky can keep its shape throughout.

Discover how to consciously adjust the angle of the bow, following the directions below.

When the student begins playing with the bow, the parent can give the direction, "Crisscross toward you" or "Crisscross away from you," to help the student find the correct bow angle.

  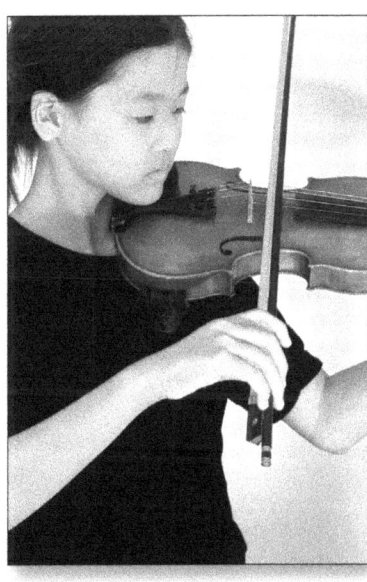

Begin with the bow aligned with the bridge. Push the frog toward the scroll while pulling the tip toward the ear.

Now do the reverse, using both the upper arm and forearm to pull the frog inward and push the tip outward.

End with the bow aligned with the bridge.

Puddle Jumps & Rainbows

Awareness of arm angle at the middle, frog, and tip. Prerequisite: Erase the Blackboard.

Puddle Jumps on the Bridge

- *Middle to Frog.* Begin in the middle of the bow, at the square of the arm. Set the bow *exactly* next to the bridge, in "bow lane one," on the A and E strings. Close any tiny gap between the bow and the bridge.

  Now hop to the frog. Again make sure the bow is *exactly* adjacent to the bridge — no gap, but not on the bridge. Practice hopping from frog to middle using quick, confident arcs.

- *Middle to Tip.* Practice hopping between the middle and tip, always exactly on the edge of the bridge. Check the bow placement after each landing. *Going to the tip is more difficult because it requires pivoting the upper arm slightly forward.*

- *Whole Bow.* Add jumps from frog to tip. These are the "rainbows." Practice jumping among all three positions.

Puddle Jumps & Rainbows in the Center Lane

Now do the exercise in the center lane (lane three). As usual, the angled visual feedback makes it difficult to assess bow straightness. The parent or teacher should help with angle corrections.

Proceed in stages: 1) puddle jumps from middle to frog, 2) puddle jumps from middle to tip; and finally 3) rainbows from tip to frog.

After each landing, check that the bow is perpendicular to the strings and in the center lane.

Introduce this exercise first with a silver-wrap bowhold. Then review the exercise once the student is playing with a frog bowhold. At this later stage, the pinky will need to release and re-curve whenever hopping to the tip of the bow.

Bow & Arrow

The velocity of the martelé bowstroke builds muscle memory for the path of the bow because the speed makes it impossible to micro-manage the bow direction midstream. The player must instead calculate the initial angle and follow its trajectory.

Violin teacher Mimi Zweig calls this bowstroke the "poof" bow. The goal is speed, not tone; an airy sound is just fine.

This exercise is not intended as a full-bow exercise. Use the upper ½ or ⅔ of the working portion of the bow.

1. Place the bow at the square of the arm.
2. Visualize the path of movement. It should follow the line of the bow.
3. Initiate the stroke with a single, quick impulse. It is only during this brief moment that energy is being added to the bow.
4. After this moment, the bow decelerates or "drifts" to a stop. The bow should end up on the string. If the bow is shooting too far, simply make the initial impulse smaller.
5. After each stroke, observe where the bow tip ended up. Is it still on the middle bow lane? Use the criss-cross motion to adjust the bow path on the next stroke to accommodate what you learned.

Ensure that all the fingers of the bow hand are loose. This will naturally loosen the wrist.

At a later time, the teacher may introduce a slight lean ("bear hug") into the index finger for tone purposes, if doing so does not compromise the looseness of the rest of the hand.

Once the stroke is mastered on D string, other strings may be introduced. The bow path is experienced differently on each string.

Crabs, Whales & Dolphins

Adjusting weight to produce an equal tone at the middle, frog, and tip.

1. **Crabs.** Make four tiny, staccato notes at the frog — almost directly under the bow hand. The frog is quite heavy so the bow must be lifted slightly so the crabs aren't too scratchy. *The crabs live under a rock on the ocean floor.*

2. **Whales.** Jump to the middle and do the same thing. A bit of "bear hug" will need to be added to achieve the same sound. Make sure the sound is large and heavy, like a whale.

3. **Dolphins.** Now do four notes at the tip. The tip is lightweight, so these notes will require a very strong "bear hug" to achieve the same sound. *The dolphins swim near the ocean surface, but they are still strong and heavy.*

Cheese Nibbles & Cheese

Adjusting weight to produce an equal tone in the upper ⅔ of the bow. Students find it easier to compare segments of the bow for equal sound, versus a single continuous note.

1. Begin at the balance point (approximately the ⅓ mark) of the bow.

2. Progress to the tip using short, staccato out-bows. All of the notes should have the same volume. The closer the student gets to the tip, the more "bear hug" they will need.

3. Finish with a continuous in-bow that returns to the starting point (balance point).

Falling Feather

Pinky strength; bow level and angle; quiet landings.

1. Begin with the bow resting on the D or A string in the middle of the bow (i.e. wherever the bow arm makes a square).

2. Lift the bow a few inches from the string, keeping the stick parallel. The teacher should choose one of the following options:
   - **Beginning**: Maintain the hand shape (with a curved pinky supporting the tip). This builds pinky strength.
   - **Advanced** (optional in Book 1): Allow the bow to "hang" from the fingers during the lift.

3. Land the bow quietly on the string.

4. Allow the knuckles to soften and flatten now that they are no longer bearing the weight of the bow. Make sure the pinky is curved. *In the "advanced" version, the arm will continue lowering even after the bow lands, restoring the original wrist-hand relationship.*

5. Do this on each string, to experience the various planes of movement.

6. When ready, practice landing at the frog and tip.

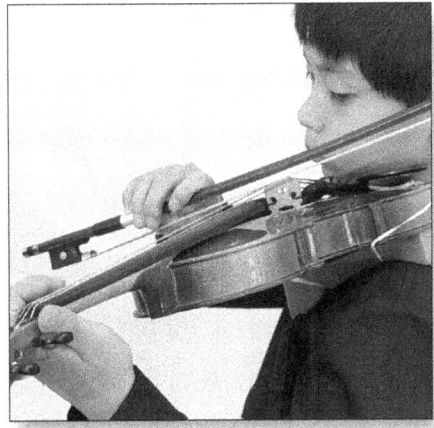

Begin with the bow resting on the D or A string, near the balance point.

Lift the bow a few inches from the string, keeping the stick parallel.

Land the bow quietly on the string.

CHAPTER 5

TECHNIQUE TRAINING

WITH THE VIOLIN & BOW

IN THIS SECTION:

Bowing Patterns

The patterns in this section should be played first on the top three strings (E, A, and D). G string may be added a week or two later, once correct bow direction is established. When the student's left hand position is correct and consistent, play the patterns below on scales. The patterns are listed in approximate order of difficulty, but the order of introduction should be customized to each student.

Teacher note: Beginning players consistently assume that "down-bow" means "going toward the bottom of the bow." To eliminate this persistent confusion, the more relatable terms "out-bow" and "in-bow" are used throughout this book. The teacher should introduce conventional terminology when the student moves into Book 2.

Demonstrations of most bowing exercises can be found on the Kaleidoscopes for Violin channel:

youtube.com/DiscoverViolin

Huckleberry Echoes

First experience using the bow, using smooth bowing within a limited bow area; getting the feel and sound of a 4-note grouping.

The student plays groups of ♩♩♩♩ echoing the parent or teacher, on E, A, D, and (optionally) G strings. Initially, the teacher or parent will "drive" the student's bow during the "Teacher play" portion. The student will "drive" during their own portion, with gentle physical guidance. When ready, the teacher models on their own violin, and the student plays independently. *The rhythm of the teacher's words can be modified as desired, as long as it follows a consistent beat and prepares the student for each new string.*

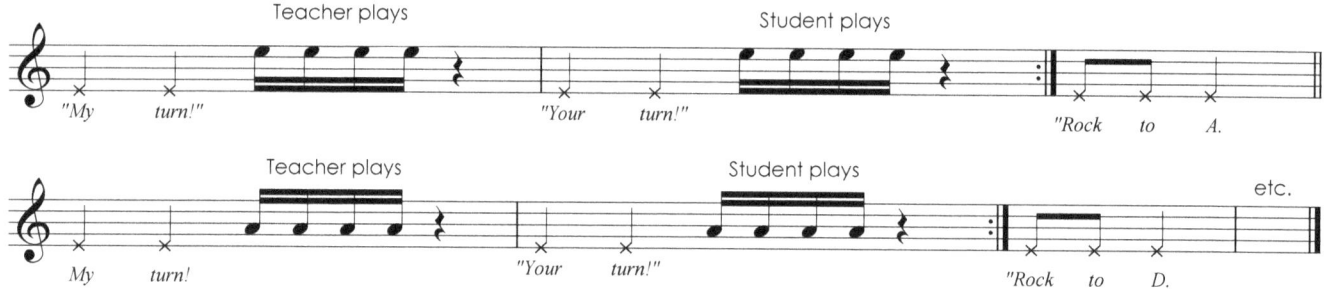

▶ Huckleberry Scale

When ready, play the pattern on a 4-note scale, ascending and descending, on D and A string. The parent or teacher will tap twice between each pattern (♪♩).

The rest can be extended to two or more beats as needed; it should be long enough for the student to prepare the next finger as well as their bow.

Chocolate Ice Cream

Straight bowing & legato bowstroke

Legato is difficult when note changes are involved; but on repeated notes it offers beginners an easy and satisfying violin-and-bow experience. Do the exercise in any part of the bow, in varying speeds; first on open strings, then on a scale. *This is simply a longer-bow version of Huckleberry! Students usually don't notice this, though.*

○ Middle ⅓ of the bow   ○ With a bear hug and relaxed arm
○ Upper ½ of the bow   ○ Full bows (at teacher's discretion)

▶ Huckleberry, Huckleberry

Relaxing the bow arm while applying weight; keeping the body grounded and stable in the presence of vigorous arm motion. Coordinating finger changes within legato.

1. *Prequel (optional): Practice playing two groups of* ♪♫♪.
2. Play the exercise on a scale.
3. Add a "bear hug" when ready. This requires engagement of the hand and forearm. The shoulder and upper arm should stay relaxed.

Popcorn Ball

Short staccato notes with good tone and clear pauses in between.

Hooked bowing is an ideal introduction to *staccato*, because full stops between notes are not a musical nuance in this stroke; they are a necessity. Each "popcorn" is a single staccato note.

Play the exercise in approximately the middle ⅓ or upper ⅔ of the working portion of the bow.

When the student is ready, a ballistic staccato can be used: 1) Use a "bear hug" to gently engage the string. 2) Move the bow in a single quick impulse, drifting to a lightweight stop.

- ○ Start with a good bowhold   ○ Listen for clean, clear stops
- ○ Re-curve the thumb and pinky when leaving the tip of the bow
- ○ Create a tiny "k" articulation at the start of each note

Option 1: Two notes per bow. *Recommended for students on a ⅛ size violin or smaller.*

Option 2: Three or four notes per bow.

▶ Popcorn Ball & Popcorn

Staccato on alternating bow direction, using hooked bows as a model.

The challenges of this exercise include: 1) Remembering how many patterns are done with each bowing; 2) Staying oriented to one's location within each pattern; and 3) Making sure that the note lengths and spaces are matched.

The teacher may adjust the number of notes in each pattern to make it easier.

Peanut Butter Cracker

This classic rhythm trains steady beat and the alternation of legato and staccato.

The physicality of this pattern is *five* legato notes, followed by *one* staccato note. A staccato marking (.) creates space *after* the note.

This pattern is practiced on open strings (four times per string) and on a 4-note scale, ascending and descending.

Raisin Bread

Full-bow skills; awareness of bow direction and bow division.

This exercise should initially use the upper ⅔ of the working portion of the bow, with a silver-wrap bowhold. Once this is mastered, expand to the full working bow. When ready, use the exercise to get used to a frog bowhold.

Use the tiniest possible amount of bow on the 🎵 ("raisin") notes. Be sure to avoid "walnuts" (staccato) and "apples" (too much bow).

All rhythmic values are approximate; the goal is good right-arm form, straight bowing, and a good tone.

▶ Upside-Down Raisin Bread

Awareness of bow direction and bow division.

This optional exercise may be introduced later in the book.

Bread & Cheese

Awareness of bow direction and bow division.

The child must stop just before the end of the bow and use a very small amount of bow on the "tiny note."

The tiny note is visibly rapid in the teacher's demo, so the child may instinctively use an energetic arm movement. However, this actually produces a lengthy (and accented) note. In reality the speed of the bow should be moderate on all three notes.

The first note ("bread") goes from the lower half to just below the tip. The "and" note (♪) is as tiny as possible, and connects to the following ("cheese") note, which returns the bow to the starting point.

The rhythmic values at this stage are a rough template; the activity is gestural in nature.

▶ Advanced Bread & Cheese

Combining and mastering hooked bows on both bow directions.

Performed with a steady beat. The ♪ should be consistent and as small as possible; its exact value is unmeasured.

Gooseberry Pie

The rapidity of the martelé bowstroke builds muscle memory for the path of the bow because the speed makes it impossible to micro-manage the bow direction midstream. The player must instead calculate the initial angle and follow its trajectory.

The Gooseberry Pie series of exercises build upon the martelé established in the Bow & Arrow exercise (see page 66).

Play these exercises in the upper 1/2 of the working portion of the bow.

The bow should shoot as fast as possible on the "goose" note (no "turtles"). The half note returns the bow to the middle.

▶ Gooseberry, Gooseberry

Speeding up the martelé impulse and fitting the "Gooseberry Pie" rhythm into a single beat, with alternating bow directions.

This exercise is introduced significantly after the original Gooseberry Pie, once the student has acquired significant bowing automaticity as well as proficiency with bow direction.

The staccato notes will no longer use a rapid martelé stroke; they should use the same amount of bow as the legato notes.

"Dots" of Sound

Ability to use a very small amount of bow; playing tiny staccato notes with good tone quality. This is useful for the staccato notes in Gooseberry, Gooseberry.

To achieve very small notes, it will help to think about moving smaller body parts (e.g. the fingers or hand) rather than larger ones (e.g. the forearm). However, this is intended only an initial introduction to this concept; the actual mechanics of finger action will be introduced on Woodpecker.

The student makes as many notes as possible on a single bow direction ... without having any "crunch tone" or "slip tone."

▶ Gingersnap, Gingersnap

A vigorous bow with two "rebound" notes. NOTE: Gingersnap is the rhythmic complement of Gooseberry. However, the third (staccato) note should not be emphasized.

Play a vigorous first note, and allow the arm movement to "coast" on the energy of the first stroke for two additional notes. There will be a decay across the three notes.

Woodpecker

The collé stroke is used here to deepen and reinforce proprioception of the bow hand and maintain the "snuggle spot" of the index finger.

1. Begin at the middle of the bow, with the bow pinky curved.
2. Holding the arm still, use only the extension of the pinky and ring finger to create the notes. (The thumb will also release.) Make sure the first finger stays on the first fold ("snuggle spot").
3. Create the up-bow by re-curving the fingers.

The pause between each four-note pattern should be as long as needed to evaluate the quality of the staccato, check and adjust the bowhold, and plan the next four strokes.

Kiwi

Variable finger pressure and bow speed (i.e., accents).

1. Begin in the middle of the bow. Lean the index into the stick.
2. Begin the note. The initial bow speed must be fast to accommodate the extra weight and avoid a crunch.
3. As soon as you hear a sound, immediately release the pressure. You will see the bow stick spring up. Simultaneously relax the arm (to smooth the bow change at the tip) and reduce the bow speed.

Once the out-bow version is mastered, the in-bow version can be introduced. This is also done in the upper half, but starts instead at the tip.

The rhythmic value of the notes are not important:

- *The first note should simply allow for a leisurely decay following the accent.*
- *The second note is as long as needed to return to the middle of the bow.*
- *The rest is as long as needed to set the next note. Later on, this preparation time will be eliminated.*

Waffles for Breakfast (and)

Introducing a rest in a novel position; continuing to develop the staccato bowstroke. NOTE: If a student is struggling with when to change notes, a version with the rest shifted to the end can be a useful prequel: ♪♪♪ ⁊

During the learning stage it may be useful to speak or do a movement during the rest (e.g. "yum!" or tapping the left thumb) to help make the rest value more concrete.

Slur Exercise

Agility and rhythmic accuracy of the left hand; dividing the bow equally; making beautiful tone in all parts of the bow; and ending a slur with a tapered staccato note. A five-note version ("do re do re do") can be introduced if desired.

This exercise can be played in a variety of keys. The last note of each pattern uses less bow and comes to a tapered stop.

Seaweed Fingers

Developing relaxed, passive movement in the bow fingers.

Play two groups of four on every note. The student can use the mirror to see if the "seaweed" motion is visible.

The motion will happen naturally if the fingers are relaxed. It is different in this way from the "flapping the wings" movement, which is purposeful.

Tonic Triad

Introduce the fundamental building block of Western harmony.

Play the tonic triad, *do mi so do' so mi do*, in any rhythmic pattern. Feel free to elongate the last note and/or add *so, do* at the end, as desired.

Ocean Tides

Shifting the weight from side to side and swaying of the body.

This uses the same bowing and rhythm as Seaweed Fingers, but the focus is on shifting the weight freely from left foot to right, creating a swaying motion in the body.

Practice the motion first without playing. The body movement should be extremely slow. When adding the scale, be sure the movement stays extremely slow. The swaying should be out of sync with the beat of the scale.

Peanut Butter String Check

Playing on two strings at a time; learning the correct, in-tune sound of the open strings played together.

At the beginning of each practice, tune the violin using a chromatic tuner. Play the "peanut butter cracker" pattern on each set of strings at least twice. If the strings sound out of tune together, use the chromatic tuner to re-adjust the pitch.

Developing a routine of playing this daily prepares the student to tune their violin without relying solely upon the tuner.

Crossing the Ocean

This pattern introduces legato bowing with a metronome, and the skill of connecting bows while crossing strings.

Play four-beat notes with the metronome at ♩=80. Strive for smooth, connected bows from frog to tip.

Left-Hand Development

Sea Serpent

Awareness of finger shape and ability to tune the 2ⁿᵈ and 3ʳᵈ finger.

Slide just the finger silently along the string, without moving the hand or arm:

1. **Silent Sea Serpent** (without the bow, in "near" position). This helps students discover how the shape of the finger must change in order to land on the finger tape.
2. **With the Bow.** This helps the student to understand and locate the physical angle for G♯ (in E major) and C♮ (in G major).

In "near" position:

In "far" position:

Sleeping Unicorn

Training the finger and hand angle for the E string.

This exercise focuses on the angle of the first finger on the E string. It can be played in "near position" or "far position."

For most students, the finger should land on the *thumb-side corner of the finger pad* for A string, and on the *tip of the finger pad* for E string.

Place a small (unicorn) eraser on the "tabletop" of the first finger. The unicorn should remain in place throughout the exercise.

At the end of the exercise, remove the unicorn and, if desired, observe the indentation created on the first finger by the string. This is the finger "tattoo." We can use this indentation to confirm whether our finger angle matched our intentions.

Near Position. Play the exercise four times.

Far Position. Play the exercise four times.

> The hand and elbow angle should be the same for E string as it is for A string. We just "close the window" of the first finger to reach the E string.
>
> Make sure the elbow does not go "behind" the violin. The base knuckle of the first finger should stay gently touching the neck.

Finger Magnets

Being aware of and accurately landing on the correct point of contact for each finger. NOTE: This exercise may also help to correct the angle of the left wrist.

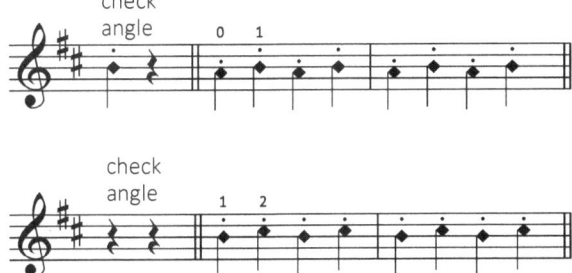

On the student's left hand, the teacher uses a magic marker to place dots: 1) on the thumb-side corner of the first and second fingers, and 2) on the tip of the third finger. *These dots are the "magnets" which will be "drawn" to the metal violin strings.*

1. **Preparation**: Place fingers 1, 2, and 3 on the "magnets." Swish the left thumb back and forth to be sure that it is relaxed.

2. Silently tap each line of the exercise, making sure to land on the "magnet" for the finger which is tapping.

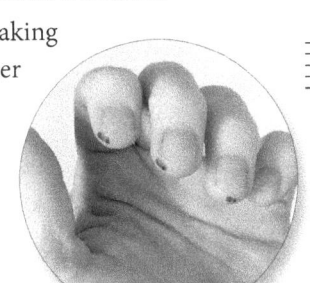

3. Play the same exercise with the bow.

4. Play the same exercise on the D string — first silently, then with the bow.

Schradieck Etude

These études build speed, tuning and agility of the left hand. See pages 20-21 in the student book for student-size print.

Teach the patterns either by reading the music (speak the solfège names out loud without the violin) or by rote using solfège.

These exercises below are patterns 1, 10, 11, and 17 from *The School of Violin Technics*, by Henry Schradieck (1846–1918). The are designed to help build a quick left hand, balanced hand frame, and consistent intonation.

Young players quickly grasp these memorable patterns, and find them intriguing and fun. Each exercise is played in A

major, on the A string. Use the 4th finger for *so*.

Novices generally pause between groups, in order to mentally process the next set. These pauses are helpful and can be retained as long as needed.

Focus on a new pattern each 4–6 weeks. There is no expectation of playing the exercises back-to-back.

1.

10.

11. Silently place all fingers in order (1, 2, 3, 4) before playing this one and the next.

17.

TECHNIQUE TRAINING

TWINKLE VARIATIONS

The goal of this stage is to fully master the previously learned bowing patterns and incorporate them into a melodic context. Students enjoy the novelty and variety of playing Twinkle in various rhythms.

The patterns below are listed in approximate order of difficulty. Patterns involving continuous activity are generally slightly harder than those with built-in processing time (i.e. longer note values).

The teacher may introduce selected Twinkle variations as soon as the student is ready. A given variation may be assigned in any of the positions or keys the student has learned.

The inclusion of long notes helps the student more easily perceive the triplet groupings. A more advanced version would consist exclusively of triplets.

APPENDIX

SONGS IN G MAJOR

Kaleidoscopes is designed so that students can play any song they like, whenever they feel ready. They do not need to ask the teacher's permission first, except where indicated.

Songs are notated below not primarily for use by students, but as a reference for parents who already read music.

If you are wanting to teach your child how to read music, please ask your teacher first. Some "traditional" ways of teaching note-reading will actually get in the way of your child's progress in developing more advanced music literacy skills.

Your child will learn the songs below in several keys, using the solfège as a transposition tool. For simplicity, the songs are notated here in just one key.

Boil Them Cabbage Down

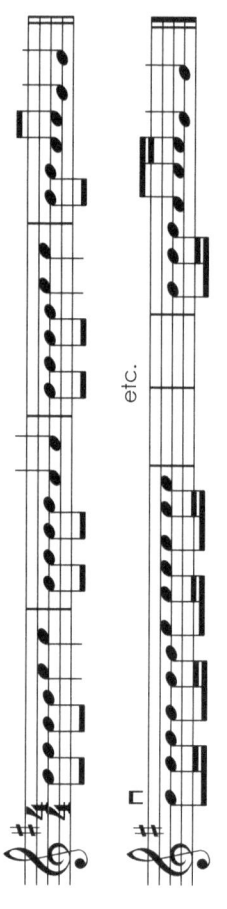

etc.

Hot Cross Buns

All My Little Ducklings

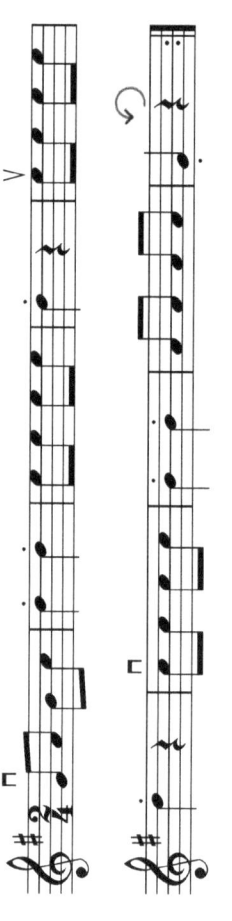

Let Us Chase the Squirrel

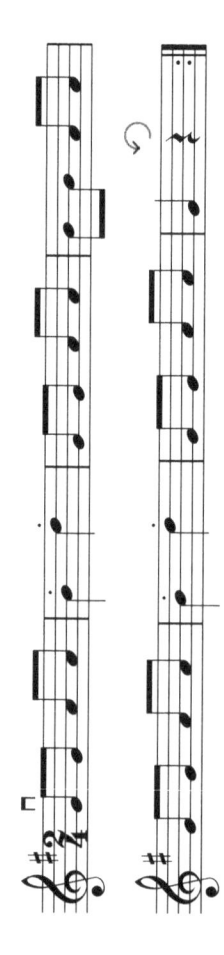

All Around the Buttercup

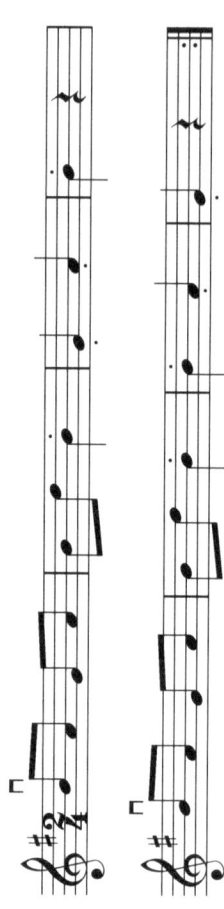

80

Mary Had a Little Lamb

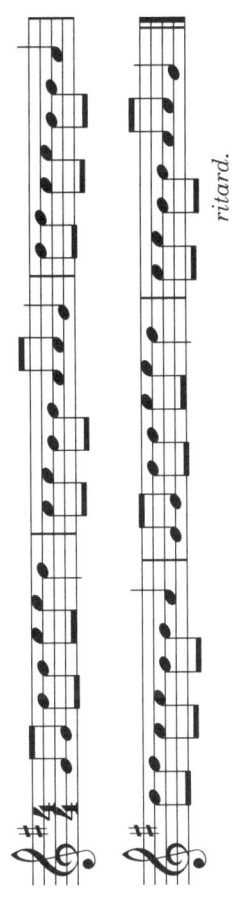

Twinkle, Twinkle, Little Star

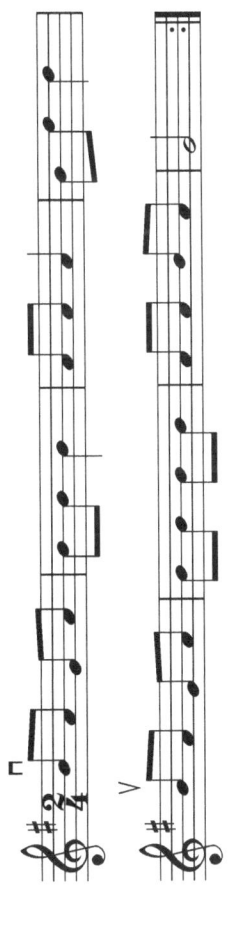

ritard.

Poor Little Kitty

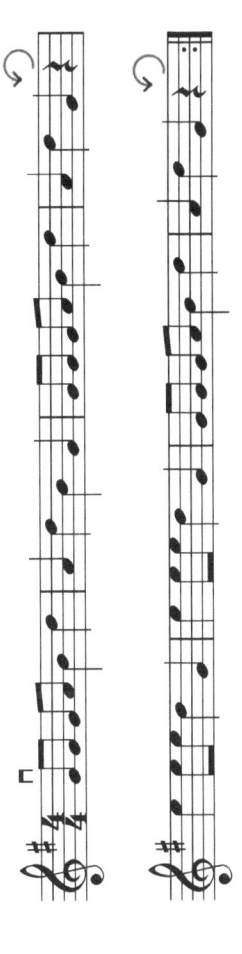

mp / f

mp / p

second time rit.

Button, You May Wander

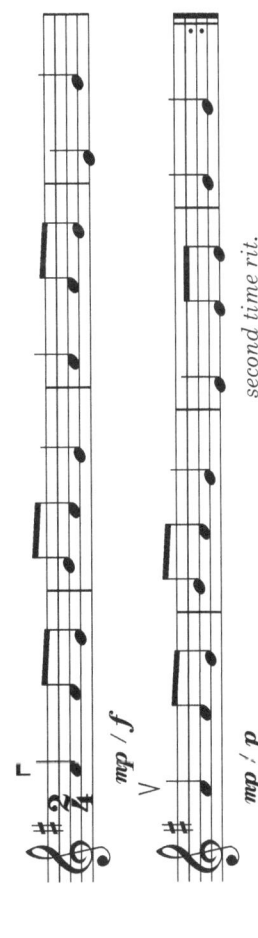

Naughty Kitty Cat

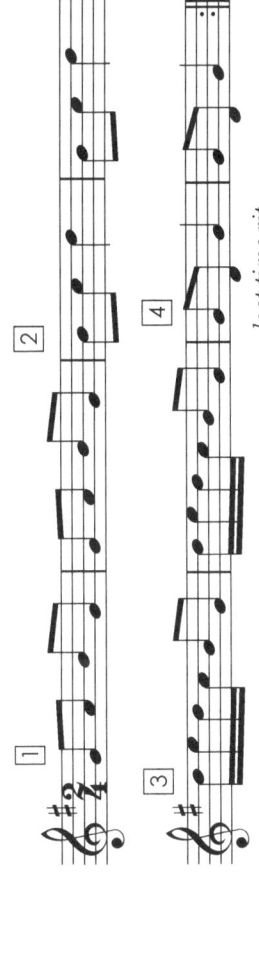

Frere Jacques

1

2

3

4

last time rit.

81

This Old Man

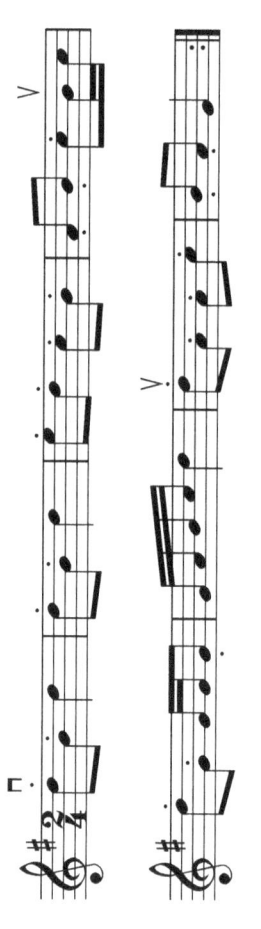

Hush-a-Bye (Arrorró, Mi Niño)

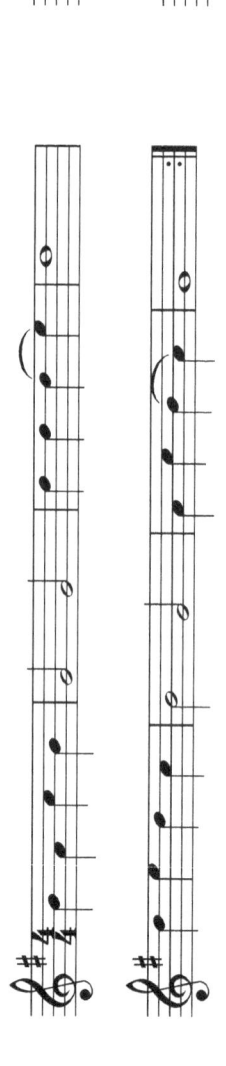

Toddy-O

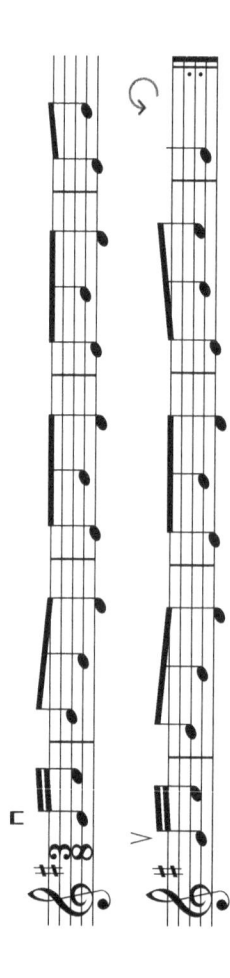

There's a Hole in the Bucket

Love Somebody (Soldier's Joy)

Reuben & Rachel

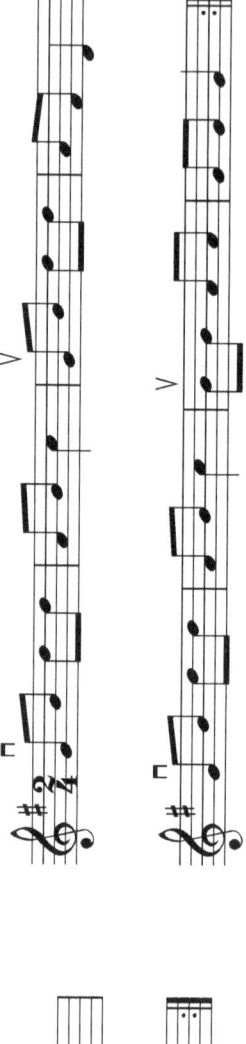

Bingo Was His Name

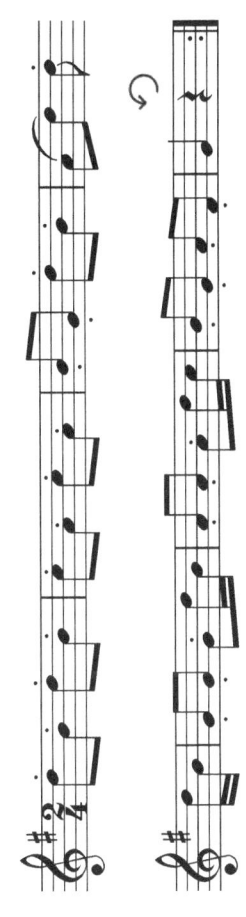

Birds' Wedding (Vogel Hochzeit)

White Coral Bells

When a student is ready to begin adding the slurs, the final slur may be omitted on the repeat in order to end out-bow.

last time rit.

Yankee Doodle

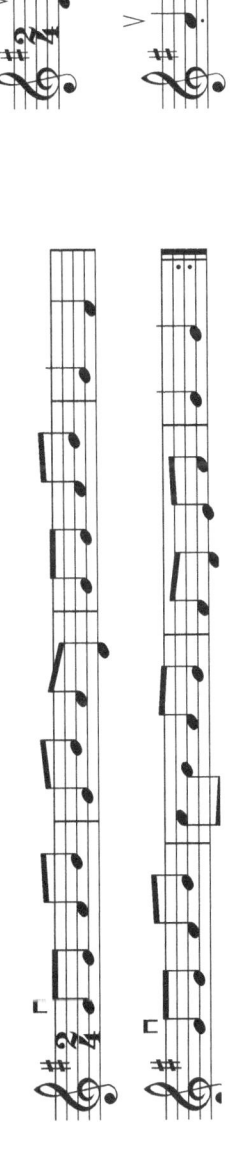

Skip to My Lou

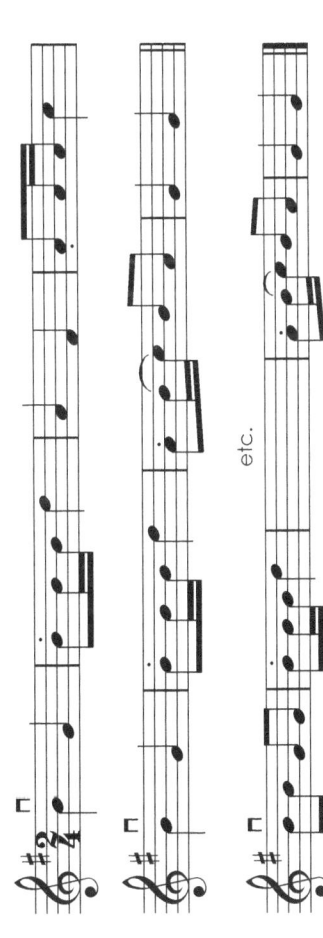

etc.

Paw Paw Patch

Keys Performed on the Recording

Voice

Track		Key
1	Hot Cross Buns	G
2	Let Us Chase the Squirrel	G
3	Boil Them Cabbage	F
4	All My Little Ducklings	F
5	All Around the Buttercup	G
6	Mary Had a Little Lamb	G
7	Poor Little Kitty	G
8	Naughty Kitty Cat	A
9	Twinkle, Twinkle	E
10	Button, You May Wander	E♭ / F
11	Frere Jacques	G
12	Arrorró, Mi Niño	E
13	There's a Hole in the Bucket	A
14	Reuben and Rachel	E
15	This Old Man	D
16	Toddy-O	E
17	Love Somebody	G
18	Yankee Doodle	B♭
19	Skip to My Lou	F
20	Paw Paw Patch	G
21	Bingo	A
22	Birds' Wedding	G
23	White Coral Bells	D

Violin

Track		Key
24	Hot Cross Buns	G
25	Let Us Chase the Squirrel	G
26	Boil Them Cabbage	A
27	All My Little Ducklings	G
28	All Around the Buttercup	G
29	Mary Had a Little Lamb	G
30	Poor Little Kitty	G
31	Naughty Kitty Cat	G
32	Twinkle, Twinkle	G
33	Button, You May Wander	G / A
34	Frere Jacques	A
35	Arrorró, Mi Niño	E
36	There's a Hole in the Bucket	G
37	Reuben and Rachel	A
38	This Old Man	G
39	Toddy-O	A
40	Love Somebody	A
41	Yankee Doodle	A
42	Skip to My Lou	G
43	Paw Paw Patch	A
44	Bingo	A
45	Birds' Wedding	G
46	White Coral Bells	G